DELLA REESE

DELLA REESE

Tanya Dean

CHELSEA HOUSE PUBLISHERS
Philadelphia

Chelsea House Publishers

Editor in Chief	Sally Cheney
Director of Production	Kim Shinners
Production Manager	Pamela Loos
Art Director	Sara Davis
Production Editor	Diann Grasse

Staff for DELLA REESE

Senior Editor	LeeAnne Gelletly
Associate Art Director	Takeshi Takahashi
Design and Production	21st Century Publishing and Communications

The Chelsea House World Wide Web address is
http://www.chelseahouse.com

First Printing

1 3 5 7 9 8 6 4 2

Library of Congress Cataloging-in-Publication Data

Dean, Tanya.
    Della Reese / Tanya Dean.
        p. cm. — (Black Americans of achievement)
    Includes filmography, discography, bibliographical references and index.
    Summary: Describes the life and career of the award-winning singer and actress,
    now famous for her role in the television show *Touched by an Angel*.
    ISBN 0-7910-6291-0 (alk. paper)
    1. Reese, Della—Juvenile literature. 2. African-American women singers—
    Biography—Juvenile literature. 3. African-American actors—Biography—
    Juvenile literature. [1. Reese, Della. 2. Singers. 3. Actors and actresses.
    4. African Americans—Biography. 5. Women—Biography.] I. Title. II. Series.

MI3930.R32 D43 2001
782.42164'092—dc21
[B]   2001032467

Frontispiece:
Della Reese, talented singer, actress, and ordained minister, has weathered prejudice and personal tragedy through a long and successful career. Her strong faith and religious beliefs have helped her appreciate good times and endure bad times. These same qualities also make her an excellent role model for living fully, yet with dignity and grace.

CONTENTS

BLACK AMERICANS OF ACHIEVEMENT

HENRY AARON
baseball great

KAREEM ABDUL-JABBAR
basketball great

MUHAMMAD ALI
heavyweight champion

RICHARD ALLEN
religious leader and social activist

MAYA ANGELOU
author

LOUIS ARMSTRONG
musician

ARTHUR ASHE
tennis great

JOSEPHINE BAKER
entertainer

TYRA BANKS
model

BENJAMIN BANNEKER
scientist and mathematician

COUNT BASIE
bandleader and composer

ANGELA BASSETT
actress

ROMARE BEARDEN
artist

HALLE BERRY
actress

MARY MCLEOD BETHUNE
educator

GEORGE WASHINGTON
CARVER
botanist

JOHNNIE COCHRAN
lawyer

BILL COSBY
entertainer

MILES DAVIS
musician

FREDERICK DOUGLASS
abolitionist editor

CHARLES DREW
physician

PAUL LAURENCE DUNBAR
poet

DUKE ELLINGTON
bandleader and composer

RALPH ELLISON
author

JULIUS ERVING
basketball great

LOUIS FARRAKHAN
political activist

ELLA FITZGERALD
singer

ARETHA FRANKLIN
entertainer

MORGAN FREEMAN
actor

MARCUS GARVEY
black nationalist leader

JOSH GIBSON
baseball great

WHOOPI GOLDBERG
entertainer

DANNY GLOVER
actor

CUBA GOODING JR.
actor

ALEX HALEY
author

PRINCE HALL
social reformer

JIMI HENDRIX
musician

MATTHEW HENSON
explorer

GREGORY HINES
performer

BILLIE HOLIDAY
singer

LENA HORNE
entertainer

WHITNEY HOUSTON
singer and actress

LANGSTON HUGHES
poet

JANET JACKSON
musician

JESSE JACKSON
civil-rights leader and politician

MICHAEL JACKSON
entertainer

SAMUEL L. JACKSON
actor

T. D. JAKES
religious leader

JACK JOHNSON
heavyweight champion

MAE JEMISON
astronaut

MAGIC JOHNSON
basketball great

SCOTT JOPLIN
composer

BARBARA JORDAN
politician

MICHAEL JORDAN
basketball great

CORETTA SCOTT KING
civil-rights leader

MARTIN LUTHER KING, JR.
civil-rights leader

LEWIS LATIMER
scientist

SPIKE LEE
filmmaker

CARL LEWIS
champion athlete

RONALD MCNAIR
astronaut

MALCOLM X
militant black leader

BOB MARLEY
musician

THURGOOD MARSHALL
Supreme Court justice

TERRY MCMILLAN
author

TONI MORRISON
author

ELIJAH MUHAMMAD
religious leader

EDDIE MURPHY
entertainer

JESSE OWENS
champion athlete

SATCHEL PAIGE
baseball great

CHARLIE PARKER
musician

ROSA PARKS
civil-rights leader

COLIN POWELL
military leader

QUEEN LATIFAH
entertainer

DELLA REESE
entertainer

PAUL ROBESON
singer and actor

JACKIE ROBINSON
baseball great

CHRIS ROCK
comedian and actor

DIANA ROSS
entertainer

AL SHARPTON
minister and activist

WILL SMITH
actor

WESLEY SNIPES
actor

CLARENCE THOMAS
Supreme Court justice

SOJOURNER TRUTH
antislavery activist

HARRIET TUBMAN
antislavery activist

NAT TURNER
slave revolt leader

TINA TURNER
entertainer

ALICE WALKER
author

MADAM C. J. WALKER
entrepreneur

BOOKER T. WASHINGTON
educator

DENZEL WASHINGTON
actor

J. C. WATTS
politician

VANESSA WILLIAMS
singer and actress

VENUS WILLIAMS
tennis star

OPRAH WINFREY
entertainer

TIGER WOODS
golf star

ON
ACHIEVEMENT

— ❧ —

Coretta Scott King

Before you begin this book, I hope you will ask yourself what the word *excellence* means to you. I think it's a question we should all ask, and keep asking as we grow older and change. Because the truest answer to it should never change. When you think of excellence, perhaps you think of success at work; or of becoming wealthy; or meeting the right person, getting married, and having a good family life.

Those goals are worth striving for, but there is a better way to look at excellence. As Martin Luther King Jr. said in one of his last sermons, "I want you to be first in love. I want you to be first in moral excellence. I want you to be first in generosity. If you want to be important, wonderful. If you want to be great, wonderful. But recognize that he who is greatest among you shall be your servant."

My husband knew that the true meaning of achievement is service. When I met him, in 1952, he was already ordained as a Baptist minister and was working toward a doctoral degree at Boston University. I was studying at the New England Conservatory and dreamed of accomplishments in music. We married a year later, and after I graduated the following year we moved to Montgomery, Alabama. We didn't know it then, but our notions of achievement were about to undergo a dramatic change.

You may have read or heard about what happened next. What began with the boycott of a local bus line grew into a national crusade, and by the time he was assassinated in 1968 my husband had fashioned a black movement powerful enough to shatter forever the practice of racial segregation. What you may not have read about is where he learned to resist injustice without compromising his religious beliefs.

He adopted a strategy of nonviolence from a man of a different race, who lived in a different country and even practiced a different religion. The man was Mahatma Gandhi, the great leader of India, who devoted his life to serving humanity in the spirit of love and nonviolence. It was in these principles that Martin discovered his method for social reform. More than anything else, those two principles were the key to his achievements.

These books are about African Americans who served society through the excellence of their achievements. They form part of the rich history of black men and women in America—a history of stunning accomplishments in every field of human endeavor, from literature and art to science, industry, education, diplomacy, athletics, jurisprudence, even polar exploration.

Not all of the people in this history had the same ideals, but I think you will find that all of them had something in common. Like Martin Luther King Jr., they all decided to become "drum majors" and serve humanity. In that principle—whether it was expressed in books, inventions, or song—they found a goal and a guide outside themselves that showed them a way to serve others instead of living only for themselves.

Reading the stories of these courageous men and women not only helps us discover the principles that we will use to guide our own lives; it also teaches us about our black heritage and about America itself. It is crucial for us to know the heroes and heroines of our history and to realize that the price we paid in our struggle for equality in America was dear. But we must also understand that we have gotten as far as we have partly because America's democratic system and ideals made it possible.

We are still struggling with racism and prejudice. But the great men and women in this series are a tribute to the spirit of the country in which they have flourished. And that makes their stories special and worth knowing.

1

AN "ANGEL" AMONG US

T HE LAST PLACE in which most people expect to see an angel is Las Vegas, Nevada. On October 16, 1999, however, dozens of angel-winged trophies were handed out at the annual Gabriel Awards. The award is named for one of the chief angels of heaven: Gabriel, a messenger from God to mankind. The award has been presented for more than 35 years to honor excellence in broadcasting. Categories include television programs, special features, short films, radio programs, and individuals who excel in their fields. It is presented by Unda-USA, an organization that recognizes and honors people and programs in broadcasting that help bring positive messages to viewers and listeners.

Each year the top award, the Gabriel Personal Achievement Award, goes to an individual whose work and career have shown outstanding leadership in the industry. The award is presented to a person whose work has touched the lives of viewers and listeners, lifted their spirits, and provided hope and a positive message. Most of the judges work in broadcasting themselves. Some previous winners of the Personal Achievement Award include Fred Rogers (*Mr. Rogers' Neighborhood*), Michael Landon (*Little House on the Prairie*), Angela Lansbury (*Murder She Wrote*), and veteran CBS news anchor Walter Cronkite.

Della at the 49th Annual Primetime Emmy Awards in 1997 where she was nominated for best supporting actress for her role in Touched By An Angel. *She has won Gabriel and NAACP awards and was nominated for a Grammy award. These awards and nominations honor Della's leadership and accomplishments in the music, broadcasting, and entertainment fields.*

At the 1999 ceremony, the award was given to another "angel" of sorts—Della Reese, who plays the angel Tess on CBS's *Touched by an Angel.* The show is also a multiple recipient of the Gabriel Award, having been honored in 1996, 1998, and 2000. On this night, Della received individual recognition. "How fitting that the angel Gabriel should come to her!" said one of the award's presenters that evening.

Standing onstage holding the golden angel, Della looked around as the audience applauded. This city was special to her. It had been 45 years since she had first come to Las Vegas. Della, already a well-known gospel singer, began performing in Vegas halls in 1954. Before she arrived, no one had ever been booked to sing gospel music there. Las Vegas was considered a sinner's town, a place for partying, hard drinking, and gambling. That did not stop Della. She knew that this door had opened so that she could bring her talent and uplifting message to the people who would come to hear her sing.

Della has been the recipient of other awards as well. She is a five-time winner of the NAACP Image Award for Outstanding Lead Actress in a Television Drama Series and has been nominated for Golden Globe and Emmy Awards. Both as the angel Tess and as a biracial woman with a message for all people, Della Reese has influenced many fans.

Viewers frequently write to *Angel* cast members to tell them how a particular episode has made a difference to them. In some cases, a show turns out to deliver just the right message at just the right time. A recovering alcoholic tells the "angels" that the show reminds her that she is not alone. Another viewer wants the cast to know that the program was the one thing that gave her hope for her mother, who was a heroin addict. People whose loved ones have died write to explain the kind of comfort the show brings. One young viewer wrote, "[N]ot all the drugs in the world can replace [God's] love."

Della as Tess, with Touched By An Angel *costar Roma Downey. Both actresses' characters are angels. People's joyful response to the show's message of hope and love is astounding—not bad for a rare program that dares to use the word "God." Della's own religious beliefs make her very happy to be part of this healthy and sincere television show.*

Della and other members of the cast find that when they are in public, people approach them easily and want to tell them very personal thoughts. Critics of the show first considered it and the characters to be "too good." They have since reconsidered their impressions. Many credit the show's charismatic cast members with offering a positive, healthy, and sincere message of hope. Some viewers who were initially concerned that the show might try to "push God down our throats" have also had changes of heart. A 19-year-old viewer who had recently lost her father to a terminal illness wrote in to say, "[A]fter seeing your

In 2000, Della also won a Family Award in the best actress category. The Family Awards honor work in family-friendly television. The singer/actress says that her mother, who died when Della was only 18, was her "angel." Nelli gave her love and support, and taught her that God should be a part of everyday life, not just on Sundays.

[episode about a terminally ill man who found peace], I realized you were simply trying to give people some hope. . . . You have won yourself a believer."

For more than seven years, Della has led her "angels" each week, offering words of wisdom and hope. As Tess, Della supervises Monica, "an angel in training," and Andrew, the angel of death. Della herself is also an ordained minister with her own church in Los Angeles. The "angel" and the actress are very much the same person. Raised in a faith-filled home, Della also has found hope and strength in messages from others—people she calls her angels. "My mother gave me that platform to stand on," she says when asked who her angels have been. "In my house, God was part of the family. It wasn't a thing we did on Sunday. It's bred in me. *Touched by an Angel* is just an affirmation for me that God has given me a place to teach what I know."

The television show gives Della the opportunity to share what she knows with millions of viewers each week. "There are some people . . . who don't have any close relationships," says Della. "Nobody to say 'God loves you and God is consciously aware that you're even on this earth.' And this show gives this, it says that." At an age when many people choose to retire, Della is still going strong. She is proud of what the show offers people, and she is committed to staying with it for a long time to come.

As a singer, actress, show host, mother, wife, minister, and friend, Della Reese has been sharing her message of hope and harmony since she was a girl. Through tough times and some life-threatening trials, Della's voice keeps issuing the same truth: "You are not alone." And today, millions are listening.

2

DETROIT'S DARLING

❦

DELOREESE PATRICIA EARLY was born on July 6, 1931, in Detroit, Michigan. She lived with her parents on the East Side in an area known as Black Bottom. Della's father, Richard Thad Early, was a steelworker and a good provider. He was handsome and well-liked in his neighborhood because, according to Della, he was a great deal of fun. Whenever someone had a party or gathering, the Early family was invited. Mr. Early gave stirring speeches and made memorable toasts. If anyone wanted to hear a story, they had only to ask Richard Early and he would weave a tale that kept everyone's attention.

Nellie Mitchelle Early, Della's mother, was the neighborhood "healer." She knew how to expertly bandage an injury and how to soothe a troubled soul. A full-blooded Cherokee Indian from Dyersberg, Tennessee, Nellie Early had long black hair, long enough for her to sit on. Because of her Native American background, she had many recipes for ointments and herbal remedies. Although she never finished sixth grade, Mrs. Early was considered the wisest woman in Black Bottom, the one nearly everyone sought for advice.

Unlike her husband, Mrs. Early was soft-spoken and quiet. She often prayed softly to herself, and she frequently told her daughter that God took a

The city of Detroit in the 1930s where Della's family owned an apartment building. Despite the dangerous neighborhood, her own world was quite safe and full of love. Her family was well-liked; her father was a fine public speaker and her mother, an American Indian, was respected as a very effective healer. Even as a little child, Della loved to show off her excellent singing, acting, and dancing abilities.

personal interest in each person and cared about each living creature. Della grew up listening to her mother talk to God as though he were in the room with them. She learned that God loved her and was with her all the time. It is no wonder that today, Della offers the same message to millions of *Touched by an Angel* viewers.

Nellie had been married twice and had five children before she wed Richard. Three daughters, Nodie, Susan, and Gladys, were from her first marriage to a man named Wiley. All lived in other states and were grown by the time Della met them when she was 12 years old. Two other siblings, Ora Mae and Rufus David (known as R.D.), lived on the west side of Detroit with their father, John Daniels. Della was six when R.D. came to live with them for a short time. Daniels came to take back R.D. a few months later. Despite having all these siblings, Della was raised as though she were an only child. That was just fine with her.

Regardless of the love and safety in the Early home, the Black Bottom ghetto was a rough area. An area just a few blocks south of Della's home was beset with drug deals, shootings, prostitution, and illegal gambling. You could get anything in Black Bottom. But the Early family stayed away from all of that. Their neighborhood seemed to be set apart from the darkness of the rest of the East Side. Perhaps it was because the Earlys were a hard-working, God-worshipping family.

The family lived next to a soap factory in a three-story, 12-unit apartment building that they owned and managed. The neighborhood had a hamburger stand, a pool hall, a drugstore, doctor and dentist offices, a deli, and a movie theater. Everything they wanted or needed was nearby. It was a tight-knit community. They watched out for each other, and Della could not venture far from an adult's watchful eye. She also knew that if she did anything wrong

the neighbors would tell her mother, or might even discipline her themselves. This was perfectly fine with Nellie and Richard.

Della and her parents were very close. Nellie often took her daughter to the movies, one of Della's favorite pastimes. As a child, she loved to watch Shirley Temple, Lena Horne, and especially Ethel Waters. Della loved the stories and the music in the movies. She was a natural actress herself.

God was a part of the family in the Reese household, and helped Della and her family keep hope in a neighborhood beset with drugs and crime. Churches with choirs like the Olivet Baptist Church gave Della the opportunity to showcase her beautiful singing voice.

When she was only three years old, she put on shows for her father. She sang, danced, and acted out parts from the movies she had seen. Her father enjoyed his daughter's performances. Della could please an audience, and she loved the attention.

Nellie, known as "Babe" to her husband, kept a spotless house and was an expert cook. Della loved the aromas of her mother's kitchen. Even though the Earlys were poor, Della's life was rich. All their needs were met; if they ran short of money or food, Babe just started praying. Soon, it always seemed, a little miracle would happen. Sometimes a neighbor would drop by with an "extra" loaf of bread to give to the Earlys. It appeared that God provided whatever Babe asked of him.

Della's family was not alone in their difficulties in keeping food on the table. The United States was in the midst of the Great Depression, brought on by the stock market crash of October 29, 1929. Businesses and banks closed, causing sharp reductions in industrial production and employment. By 1932, more than 12 million Americans—about one-fourth of all workers—were unemployed. Money was scarce, and what was available was needed for essentials such as food and shelter.

By 1933 the economy had almost completely collapsed. Franklin Delano Roosevelt, the newly elected president, had promised the American people a "New Deal," a program that offered the hope of restoring the country's economy and boosting job rates by establishing new federal programs to aid Americans.

Detroit was especially hard-hit by the Depression. That is because Detroit was, and still is, a major manufacturing hub, known in particular for its automobile production. But few people could afford to buy a car in the 1930s. It was hard enough just to buy food. Growing up during the Depression, Della learned to appreciate the basic things in life:

a warm home, good food, and close family. She saw her parents help people who were less fortunate than they were and learned that such values were an important part of living a good life.

Della's mother was blessed with many intangible gifts. One of the most unusual was her ability to know if danger were near. She had "impressions," or feelings, about people. She believed that God gave her this gift so she could keep her family safe. Nellie's faith was the strength of the family.

The economic slowdown of the Great Depression in the 1930s forced many people out of jobs and onto 'bread lines' where they waited to receive free food from charities. The Depression made Della appreciate the few things she had: a home, food, and family. Her parents helped many people who couldn't even fill those basic needs.

It held them together during tough times. When Della was three years old, she was inflicted with a disease called rheumatic fever, which causes painful swelling of the joints, especially the knees and ankles. The swelling can cause great physical damage.

Della developed a severe case of rheumatic fever, and doctors warned Nellie that Della would never walk again. But Nellie would not accept the verdict. She wrapped Della's legs in hot and then cold towels, somehow "knowing" it would help heal her child. She massaged Della's legs over and over and talked to God all the while. She asked God to make Della's legs perfect again. Within a few weeks, Della's health improved. She got better with each passing day. Della has never since had pain or problems with her legs.

During her recovery, Della made a new friend named Bernice White, a young lady in her twenties who lived in the Earlys' building. She spent time teaching Della the alphabet and how to count. Della was a quick learner, and Bernice continued to teach the youngster. Della was able to read by the time she was four. She loved books. Bernice took Della to the nearby elementary school when Della was only four and a half years old. The administrators at the school were impressed by Della's abilities and told her she was ready for the first grade. She started school the following week.

Della's parents were pleased that their daughter was ready for school. Nellie had impressed upon her daughter the importance of education. No one in the family had graduated from high school, and Nellie wanted Della to be the first. Della did well academically and developed a love of reading, but her greatest joy was singing. Nellie and Della regularly attended the Olivet Baptist Church in their community. By the time Della was five, she was already a soloist in the children's choir. At six, she sang solos at the close of church services, and even performed with the choir on a radio program. The entire neighborhood was proud of Della's accomplishments; in fact, her very first concert was for her neighbors, whom she charged 25 cents each to hear her sing. She was an instant hit.

3

ON TOUR
WITH THE "QUEEN"

◆

The Clara Ward Singers, *photographed here in 1959, and several other gospel singers visited Della's church in Detroit in the 1940s. Gospel is a joyful music that talks about the faith and hope needed in life, and is usually joined with a piano, organ, and other instruments. These singers had a strong effect on the young Della.*

THE EARLY FAMILY was a tight circle of three: father, mother, and daughter. Little Deloreese was Richard and Nellie's only child together. However, Della knew that she had older brothers and sisters who did not live there. That changed when she was six, and eight-year-old R.D. appeared at the Early house. Nellie's second husband, John Daniels, had brought R.D. to live with his mother. No one knew he was coming; Daniels had simply decided that R.D. needed his mother. Nellie was happy to see her only son, and Richard accepted the boy into his home as if he were his own.

Suddenly, Della had an older brother. She adored him—most of the time. Della quickly had to learn to share things: her home, her parents, and even neighborhood friends and acquaintances. In all the usual ways, R.D. and Della were like most brothers and sisters. They played and teased each other and got into a few fights. But Della loved having her brother around so much that no one was more upset than she was when R.D.'s father returned to take his son back home only three months later.

Just as Daniels had shown up unannounced to drop off R.D., he now came back, gathered up R.D. with all of his new things, loaded everything in his car, and disappeared down the street. Richard, Nellie, and Deloreese could only stand and watch, stunned by R.D.'s abrupt departure. Later that year, the same thing happened all over again: Daniels dropped off R.D., then picked him up after a short time and took him home to his place on the other side of Detroit. However, the second time, Nellie didn't let R.D.'s father take any of the new things with him. She didn't do it to hurt R.D. Nellie wanted her son to know that his things would be waiting for him if and when he returned.

Della, who knew nothing about her mother's second husband, soon learned why her mother was no longer married to Daniels. The second time he came for R.D., he also tried to cause trouble for Nellie. An abusive man, R.D.'s father began yelling at Nellie, greatly upsetting her. Della heard what was happening and she ran to the kitchen. She took a large knife from a drawer and headed for R.D.'s father. When Nellie saw her angry daughter coming toward Daniels, she grabbed the knife. Daniels left hastily with R.D. It would be many years before the Early family would see R.D. again, and that was only because the teenaged boy sneaked away from his father's house on weekends so he could spend time with Nellie, Richard, and Della.

Della was an easygoing child most of the time, but she had to learn quickly to develop a tough side to survive 12 years in the East Detroit school system. It took only one incident to settle that issue. When she was in the fifth grade, Della had some trouble with two bullies, girls who were much bigger than she was and who delighted in intimidating other children. Della usually tried to ignore them and stay out of their way. Then one day, the girls began insulting Della's mother. Della decided it was time to fight. She grabbed one girl's hair, wrapped it around her hand, and dragged her around the schoolyard. She was expelled from school and strongly disciplined by Nellie when she got home. Nellie would not tolerate her daughter fighting, even if it were to defend the honor of a family member.

Many of the students at Della's Detroit school had grown up in abusive environments and often got into trouble. The schools could be terrifying places to be. Not everyone wanted to learn, but often, the bullies picked on the kids that did. After her fight with the two girls, Della learned that fighting in school was not acceptable. She knew she was there to get an education. She was determined to focus on her studies and not worry so much about those around her.

During those years, the neighborhood church was a haven for Della. She sang in the children's choir and stayed very active in other ways as well. However, when she was 12, she began to feel that Olivet Baptist Church was not where she wanted to be. She was a bright child, and had many questions. Not all of her questions had easy answers. Della always wanted someone to explain things to her that were confusing. For example, Nellie had taught Della that God was loving and kind. As a result, Della had trouble understanding the darker side of religion—things like sin and punishment. The people she had looked to for guidance had no helpful answers. Some even spoke harshly to Della for asking about such things. After a while, Della began to feel as though she would never get the answers she sought at Olivet Baptist Church.

Around that time, a new place of worship called the Church of Our Faith had begun holding meetings in town. It was an interdenominational church, which meant that people from all backgrounds and faiths were welcome to attend services and join the community. The new church intrigued Della. The idea of going to a more diverse place seemed right to her.

One Sunday, Della visited the Church of Our Faith. She immediately felt at home, especially when the preachers talked about a loving God rather than a punishing one. The two pastors, Reverends Barnes and Travis, joyfully taught the congregation about God. Della joined the church after her second week attending services. Nellie continued to attend Olivet, but agreed that Della's new church was just as good a place for her daughter to serve and love God.

The Church of Our Faith had a "Young People's Church" with its own offices, services, and choir. Della joined the choir right away and before long she was named director. She and the other teens had a wonderful time during services, and the church activities kept them so busy that many of them stayed off the streets and out of trouble. Reverend Travis, the youth pastor, made everyone feel loved and special. Della felt safe asking him the questions she had not been allowed to ask at Olivet Baptist. Reverend Travis never discouraged Della's curiosity, and he assured her that her deep questions and careful thoughts were good. Della's confidence and faith flourished as a result.

Many well-known gospel groups were guest performers at the Church of Our Faith. Singers such as James Cleveland, Wynona Carr, Thomas Dorsey, and the Clara Ward Singers stopped by when they toured Detroit. Gospel music was quite popular in the 1940s, and though it originated in the South, its traditions were carried north during the widespread migration of blacks around the time of the Great Depression. The expressive, powerful music was nearly unique to African Americans, who sang and performed it with great emotion and physical involvement. The roots of gospel music are in an even earlier form of African-American music, a song type known as a spiritual. This form gave slaves a means to express their sorrow and anguish over their earthly situations and their hope in a better life to come.

The similarities between spirituals and gospel songs are few. Spirituals are usually songs of sorrow, while gospel singing is a joyful type of music. Most spirituals are performed without musical instruments, while gospel music depends heavily on piano and organ accompaniment. Spirituals are simple songs

that are easy to learn and sing because of their basic harmonies and rhythms. Gospel music can be quite complex, especially because it allows singers to improvise as they perform. And while traditional spirituals focus largely on Old Testament tales, gospel music emphasizes the "good news," the meaning of the word "gospel" itself.

The gospel music of the 1930s was based for the most part on a man called the Father of Contemporary Gospel Music, Thomas Dorsey. His music was sung with so much emotion and fervor that many churches refused to include it in their services,

Thomas A. Dorsey, the Father of Contemporary Gospel Music, shown in 1959. His music was even more different from black spirituals, and the 'jubilant noise' was considered too rowdy for some churches. Gospel continued to become more popular and people began recording and purchasing its music records in unheard of numbers.

believing that it was too uncontrolled, too emotionally charged. By the 1940s, however, gospel quartets and groups of various numbers began organizing and traveling across the country, singing as guests in various churches. As the popularity of the message and the style grew, so did the demand for this music and its performers. One of the most popular touring gospel singers of that time was Mahalia Jackson.

Mahalia Jackson was known as the "Queen of Gospel." In July 1944, Jackson and her group came to sing at the Church of Our Faith. Many gospel groups had performed at Della's church, but this one was different. She was especially excited about hearing this legendary singer. Della also was excited about having Mahalia listen to her sing. Always ready to perform, she was determined to make a good impression. Because she was the director of the youth choir, 13-year-old Della sang backup with Mahalia and her group.

The first evening was particularly special for Della. She opened the service by singing a solo of "Christ Is All," with the choir as backup. This was Della's chance to shine. The young girl started singing softly yet strongly, eventually building in volume and expression until she "tore it down" with great energy and vocal power.

Now it was Mahalia's turn. The building was filled with people, despite the intense heat. Paper fans waved back and forth across the rows of worshippers. When she got to the front of the building Mahalia praised the choir as the best she had ever heard. Then she began to sing. Song after song, Mahalia and her group led the congregation. People were clapping, dancing, and waving their arms to the rhythm. The heat became unbearable. At one point, Mahalia's lead soprano fainted and had to be carried to an adjoining room.

After the service, a doctor examined the woman and discovered that she was six months pregnant. All agreed that she shouldn't continue the tour. Mahalia

Gospel singer Mahalia Jackson, the Queen of Gospel, sings on stage in Washington DC, 1950s. She also performed at Della's church. Della impressed Mahalia enough with her singing that she was asked to join the tour to replace a sick performer. This was the beginning of a strong and trusting friendship. Mahalia taught Della about singing, about faith, and about life.

and her group were leaving in two days and needed to find another singer quickly. She decided that the soprano replacement should be none other than Deloreese Early, the teenager who "tore down" the room when she sang.

Della was thrilled. Della's mother was not. Reverend Travis, the youth pastor, and Mahalia accompanied Della to her parents' home to ask Nellie for permission to allow her daughter to tour. After explaining everything to Nellie, Mahalia promised that she would personally take care of Della. Then she left Nellie so she could think and pray about the idea. Della went to bed that night feeling anxious about the outcome. She knew it would be a great experience and also knew the family could use the money she would earn. But she also knew that her mother was not going to let Della go without talking to God about it first.

The next morning, Della got up early and helped

her mother prepare breakfast. She waited and waited for her mother to start the conversation about leaving with Mahalia. Finally, Nellie told her daughter that God had not said "no." That meant that Nellie had to make the decision herself. Looking at Della intently, Nellie made her daughter promise that she would do her best and be her best before God. Della quickly agreed. Nellie's final statement on the matter was simple: she would pray daily for her daughter until she returned safely home. Mrs. Early knew the dangers that might face the group as they toured a country that was often torn apart by racism. But her faith in God was greater than her fear of the prejudice and hatred she would encounter in the South.

Della knew about racism, too. On June 20, 1943, race riots broke out in Detroit. People from the South who had suffered during the Depression came north to find work that paid well. More than 300,000 Southerners, black and white, moved north in the early 1940s. Racial tensions simmered as whites and blacks competed for the few available jobs. In the South, life was clearly marked by signs of white and black—segregation that kept blacks "in their places." The North was different, however. Although there may have been less overt racism, it was still evident.

First Lady Eleanor Roosevelt tried to set an example for whites in America. Believing that everyone should have equal opportunities in this country, she invited people of all races and all walks to life to be guests at the White House. Visitors were rich and poor, black and white, young and old. Mrs. Roosevelt was especially sensitive to the causes of women and minorities. The First Lady helped open the door to black singers across the country when she invited Marian Anderson, one of the most well-known black singers of the time, to sing "America" on the steps of the Lincoln Memorial.

Despite the good efforts of people like Eleanor Roosevelt, race riots flared across the nation during

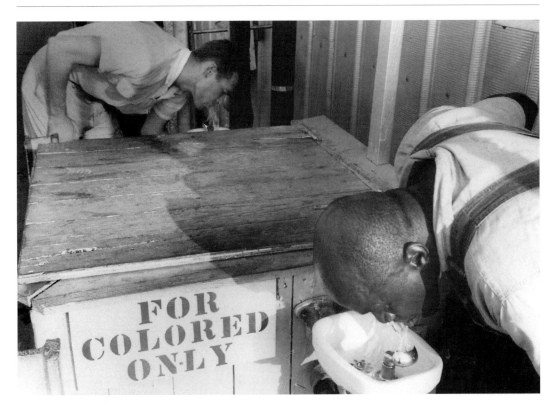

the 1940s. A two-day riot in Detroit on June 20 and 21, 1943, left 35 people dead, 600 wounded, and thousands jailed. One of the 35 dead was Della's cousin, a young man nicknamed Junior, who was killed by four white men who held him underwater at Belle Isle Park, just a mile from Della's home, until he drowned. Even as the family grieved over his unnecessary death, they knew it could just as easily have been one of them.

Keenly aware of these dangers, Della left home with Mahalia Jackson in July 1944, just a year after Junior's death. Della listened and learned as Mahalia taught her how to "stay in her place" while in the South. Sometimes Mahalia had to be even tougher on Della than Nellie had been. Thirteen-year-old Miss Early was used to being outgoing, and this type of behavior was new and difficult to learn. At first she had to be reminded often of what not to do, where not

A "For Colored Only" sign on a water fountain in the South during the 1950s. Della met with such signs and restrictions of racial prejudice for the first time on her tours with Mahalia's group. It was hard for Della to 'stay in her place.' She would encounter similar limitations, simply because of the color of her skin, throughout most of her life.

to go, and what not to say. For example, at the very first place the group stopped for dinner in the South, Della almost went in through the "wrong" door—the front door, which was clearly marked "whites only." Some places would not feed blacks at all, but those that did only served blacks via a back entrance or window, and they could not eat inside the building.

Although it was difficult and demeaning, Della learned to be quiet and pay attention to these strange differences. She knew that everyone was counting on her to do her part. They had to watch out for each other. Segregation was a normal way of life for blacks in the South. Even so, Della was never comfortable there. She learned a disturbing truth: that who you were was not nearly as important as your skin color. Even someone as respected and talented as Mahalia Jackson was simply another African American to most whites in Georgia, Arkansas, Virginia, and the other southern states they passed through.

Even a few southern church leaders tried to cheat Mahalia and her group out of their earnings. After having collected money from the people who came to see the performance, a promoter sometimes disappeared with the money. When that happened, Mahalia would tell the people who had paid about what had happened, as a means of gathering support and demanding fair treatment. Promoters on the tour soon learned that Mahalia was not to be cheated. She stood up for herself and her group, letting the congregation know that she was personally responsible for the care of her group, especially the young ones like Della who depended on the money for food. Finally, Mahalia made arrangements to be paid before she would perform, reducing the chance that she and her group would have to leave a town with no money for food or travel.

Despite all the negatives of touring in the South, Della loved the music. When the group sang, life was simple again and full of hope. Young Della sang each note with joy and gratitude. She knew that God had placed her with this group and that she was fulfilling her promise to her mother to be and do her very best.

Finally, it was time for the group to head north again. The last performance of the tour was in Chicago, Illinois. This was Mahalia Jackson's town. Several neighborhoods and churches came together to set up a big tent for the performance. Chairs were lined up for the many who were expected. The excitement over this final performance was electric. Mahalia was home, the singers were home, and the people were ready. For all these reasons the stage was set for great things to happen. It had been a long summer, and now the time to celebrate had come.

Della was the opening soloist. Knowing this was her last big moment of the season, Della sang her best. People responded enthusiastically, shouting, "Amen! Hallelujah! Sing it, child!" One of those voices belonged to Mahalia Jackson herself. Thrilled with the attention and the chance to show off, the teenager kept going. The congregation stayed with her, getting more and more caught up in the music. By the time she finished, Della felt as if she had out-sung the best of the best. Then it was Mahalia's turn.

As the Queen of Gospel sang, something changed. The atmosphere calmed down, but somehow also became more intensified. What was the difference? Della wondered. What she didn't know at the time was that she had just been performing. Mahalia on the other hand, was worshipping. Her music started inside of her and was directed upward. The people followed, moving from the "show" that Della had offered to the "real thing" that Mahalia inspired. Mahalia had connected. "She was worshipping God, and I was showing off," says Della about that night. It would take Della two summers before she came to understand the difference—that "gospel music is not a performance; it's a God thing."

4

FINDING HER OWN WAY

.♦.

A beautiful Della in 1957. Mahalia had taught her to 'fill yourself up with whatever it is you're singing about,' in other words, to believe in herself, the song, and its subject. Della used this same faith, following her mother's death, to get through tough times as a truck driver, and then as an abused wife.

DURING HER THIRD summer with Mahalia Jackson, Deloreese Early turned 15. The glamour of touring and singing in front of different people week after week was wearing thin. By the end of the summer, Della's attitude about this routine was shaken when, out of nowhere, a new talent emerged. A young girl sitting in a congregation in Virginia sang like an angel, and Mahalia took notice, just as she had when she first heard Della sing. As Mahalia spoke with the girl and her mother, Della smoldered with jealousy. The lesson about showing off had finally arrived.

Later that evening, Mahalia had a stern talk with Della. For nearly three summers, Della's focus had been on herself—how well she could sing and how lucky the group was to have her along. Now Mahalia reminded her that her singing was supposed to be about God, not about who could sing better. "You're not in competition," the Queen of Gospel told her young protégé. "You're in God's service; you're not the only one who can do it, there is someone who can do it different, and maybe even better. Just be glad that He called you, but always remember you are not the only one He called." Della listened, really listened, and she heard an angel's message telling her it was time to grow up. She was special, but so was everyone else.

In later years, Della used Mahalia's wisdom to help her in all her performances. "Fill yourself with whatever it is you're singing about and then let your listeners join you there," Della says now. Eventually Della was able to tell Mahalia just how much she had influenced her life. The young singer thanked the Queen of Gospel for guiding her during those years. Mahalia Jackson responded, "Of all the gospel singers I have sponsored or taught, you are the only one who has given me credit. You have thanked me the best way anyone could."

Deloreese Early graduated from Northeastern High School in 1948 at 16 years old. Nellie Early attended the graduation ceremony, living to see the fulfillment of one of her dreams—a child of hers had earned a high school diploma. Della worked hard in high school and did very well. Because she had been such a good student, she felt ready to move on to college after graduation.

In the fall of 1948 she began her college studies at Wayne State University in Detroit. She thought she'd like to become a psychiatrist, but it wasn't long before she realized that going to college was not an easy thing for a young and impoverished black woman. She felt out of place. When Della found out how many years of schooling she'd need to become a psychiatrist, she grew discouraged and gave up on the idea. Della knew that school would be hard enough, but she also realized that being black and female compounded the difficulty of reaching her goals. Added to that was her father's opinion that college was a waste of time and money for her. But Nellie believed otherwise, and she argued that Della should stay in college and keep pressing on. Della listened to her mother.

During that time, Della began singing with professional choirs in the Detroit area. One of them, the Original Hutchins Gospel Trumpeteers, was known as one of the finest in the country. This kept

her active in the gospel music scene and allowed her to do what she loved most—perform. One evening in 1949, Della spent a day with her mother before heading out for practice with the Trumpeteers that evening. Della remembers that as a special day, one in which she and her mother talked about important things like marriage and life. They acted silly and laughed, like two sisters playing together. Della inhaled her mother's special aroma of vanilla, cold cream, and spices as they enjoyed dinner together. Then Marie and George Waters, an older couple who also were part of the Trumpeteers, stopped by to pick up Della for choir practice.

Della attended Wayne State University in 1948, where she thought she would study to become a psychiatrist. She soon found that going to college was not an easy task for a young and impoverished black woman.

After practice, Della got a painful headache and began to cry uncontrollably. She told her friends that she wanted to go home, but, not wanting to leave so early, they asked her to wait a bit. By 11:00 P.M., Della was in so much pain that she threatened to take a bus home by herself. Marie and George said their goodbyes and took the young woman home. As soon as Della stepped out of the car and headed upstairs to the apartment, she knew something was wrong.

Louise, the neighbor across the hall, heard Della come in. She told her that Nellie had fallen down some stairs and that Della's father took Nellie to the hospital. Richard told Louise to stay with Della until he got home. Della watched out the window and waited for her father. When he finally did arrive, Della knew by the way he was walking that something was very wrong. She met him in the hallway and he told her the bad news—Nellie had had a stroke, a serious condition caused by blood vessels bursting in the brain. Damage to the brain can be minimal or life-threatening, depending on what part of the brain the injury has affected. Each stroke patient's recovery is different. Richard and Della had no choice but to wait and see how Nellie fared.

The next day Della went to visit her mother. Nellie was lying in her hospital bed, still unconscious. Della looked for signs of recovery, and she was heartened when her mother's cheeks seemed to blush with color when she spoke to her. She even thought she had seen Nellie smile a little. Certain that this was good news, Della went home to clean the apartment, hopeful that her mother would recover and come home soon. Unfortunately, it was not to be. Later that afternoon her father came home to tell Della that her mother had died.

Della cried for two days. She was inconsolable, and rarely emerged from her room. When Della was all cried out, she knew it was time to comfort her father. Everyone was astonished when they saw Della emerge: in just two days, a streak of the young woman's hair had turned completely gray.

There was a huge turnout at Nellie's funeral. She had been loved and respected by many people. As Della and her father adjusted to Nellie's death, Della realized that she needed to make some changes. She was unhappy in college, and decided not to return. Della knew that Richard could never take care of himself the way her mother had, so for the time being she planned only to stay home and care for her father.

But four months later, when Della got up to make breakfast as usual, she was shocked to find a stranger in the kitchen cooking breakfast for Richard. Della's father had found another woman. Furious with the thought that her mother could be so easily replaced, Della packed her belongings in a trunk. Her father did not try to stop her. With only 13 cents in her pocket, 17-year-old Deloreese Early left home.

For a short time Della stayed with a woman in the neighborhood named Mrs. Aikens. The young girl soon grew fond of the older woman. Della sang gospel songs to her while she helped with the house chores. Mrs. Aikens encouraged Della to think about making singing her life's work. Della hadn't given much thought to the idea of singing for a living.

After a while, Della felt it was time to leave Mrs. Aikens and find her own way. She rented a room from one of Mrs. Aikens's friends for seven dollars a week. To come up with the money, Della had to sell her trunk and many of her belongings. Still, she only had 32 dollars in her purse and knew it would not last long. It was more important than ever that she put her faith in God, and she believed that he would take care of her now that she was on her own. With that in mind, she began to look for a job.

Even though the Early family never owned a car, Della had learned to drive. Her Michigan driver's license became her ticket to a good job—as a truck driver. Della drove from Detroit to Toledo, Ohio, several times a week to deliver fruit and vegetables. Long nights and hundreds of miles earned her a respectable 100 dollars a week. Della also continued singing and was hired as director of two choirs in the Detroit area, which earned her another 50 dollars a month.

Financially, Della was doing fairly well. But she now felt she had no family, and the 18-year-old missed the closeness she had once had with her parents. One evening, she saw George and Marie Waters, the couple she had been with the evening her mother had been taken to the hospital. When they heard of Della's situation, they invited her to come and live with them for free. Della knew that her friends lived in a small, three-room apartment with their son and a gentleman who was the pianist for the Trumpeteers. Surely there was not room for one more person. Marie disagreed, so Della decided to give it a try. It was just what she needed. Soon the entire group grew very close.

Without the expense of paying rent, Della was able to give up her trucking job and focus her energy on the choirs. She continued to sing with the Trumpeteers, too. The group was becoming more popular and was developing a name in the area. Della also needed to find a church, so she went with Marie and George Waters to Detroit's New Liberty Baptist. Della became good friends with the reverend's wife, Earnestine Rundless. She became a positive role model for young Della.

Earnestine and Della sang lead together in the church choir. When Della was asked to become the choir director, she gave up her directorships at the other churches. The choir at New Liberty was extremely talented. When Reverend Rundless started a church-based radio program, Earnestine and Della put together a small group to perform during his broadcast. Because the reverend's program

Della joined the New Liberty Baptist church where she met Reverend Rundless and his wife, Earnestine. Together, Earnestine and Della put together a group called the Meditation Singers that performed on the reverend's church-based radio station; their refreshing gospel style made them very popular.

was called "Moments of Meditation," the group was named the Meditation Singers. It was made up of Della, Earnestine, Marie and George Waters, De Lillian Mitchell, Early Moore, and Emory Radford.

Almost immediately, the wildly popular group was in great demand. Churches and organizations in Detroit and Pontiac, Michigan, scheduled them to sing. Soon requests came from Chicago, Illinois; Cleveland and Toledo, Ohio; Pittsburgh, Pennsylvania; Buffalo, New York; and Richmond, Virginia. No one sang like the Meditation Singers. Most groups had one lead singer and the other members sang backup. The Meditation Singers had two leads, Della and Earnestine. As one would lead, the other would act as what they called a "second lead," while the rest of the group sang harmony. It was an exciting time for gospel music and the Meditation Singers had a refreshing and new style. Years later, the group was inducted into the Gospel Singers' Hall of Fame.

Life was going well for Della. She enjoyed her church, her friends, and her singing. Soon she met a young man who would become her husband. After only six months of dating, Della married Vermont Taliaferro, a fellow church member. Before the wedding, Della returned to visit her father and ask him to attend the wedding. The two mended their torn relationship, and that week, Richard Early walked his daughter down the aisle.

At first the newlyweds were happy. Vermont was a good provider, working two jobs at local factories. He showered Della with gifts, including the best clothing and jewelry she had ever owned. A few months later, however, things began to change. Vermont, normally gentle and kind, became controlling and violent. Della grew to fear him. She never knew how he would behave toward her—as a loving husband or as an abuser. Eventually Vermont became so violent that he beat Della. One time he beat her so badly that she spent five days in a hospital. Two years after saying, "I do," Della said, "No more." She left Vermont and moved back in with George and Marie Waters.

Della used her driver's license to land another job, this time as a taxi driver. Unwilling to let his wife leave, Vermont tried to follow Della, so she looked for other work where she would be safe. One night she noticed a job posting for a switchboard operator at the Carlton Plaza Hotel. In those days, telephone services in public service buildings were connected at one central location, a switchboard, which was monitored by an operator who connected the calls directly to the rooms. Della had never worked a switchboard before, but she convinced the hotel manager that she could learn. She moved into a small room there and earned $50 a week, of which half went to paying for the room.

Della enjoyed working at the Carlton. It was one of the two best black hotels in Detroit. She met many interesting people there and was enjoying her life again. During the week she worked at the switch-board, and on the weekends she sang with the gospel groups. She knew that God was continuing to take care of her. She also knew that she had the skills and determination to take care of herself. Finally, Della and Vermont officially divorced. On her own again, Della knew it was time to think about how she could have the kind of life she really wanted for herself.

5

BRINGING DOWN
THE HOUSE

꧁꧂

WHILE WORKING AT the Carlton, Della became close friends with Dorothy Smith, one of the best-liked waitresses there. Dorothy also worked as a waitress at some of the other establishments in Detroit. Dorothy was Della's biggest fan. She believed in Della, and let everyone else know about her, too. Dorothy told her customers that Della was one of the best singers around and encouraged them to ask her to sing for them.

Whenever Della went to one of Dorothy's places to "hang out" while Dorothy worked, customers often did request Della to sing. After playfully protesting, Della eagerly performed. The customers were never disappointed. This was not the church crowd that Della was used to singing for. People requested popular songs of the day, and Della loved singing songs like "April in Paris" as well as her own favorites. Mixing gospel and secular songs in the same performance did not bother Della. When she sang, she sang from her heart no matter what the type of music.

As a result of these impromptu performances, Della began getting work at some local bars. It was during one of these gigs that Deloreese Early became Della Reese. In 1952 or 1953 (she can't remember exactly), the owner of a small nightclub tried to put the name "Deloreese Taliaferro" on his tiny marquee.

After singing only in churches and for friends, singing in night-clubs was a new challenge, paid better money, and, as always, was an even bigger chance to show off. Della enjoyed entertaining people and making them laugh. She knew that simply singing for these people who had made bad choices would not make her become like them.

47

This was the name Della had been performing under since her marriage to Vermont. The man only put up her first name. Then he split the name in two, slightly adjusting the spelling on the first half. There, in clear letters on the marquee, the young black singer saw her new name: Della Reese. She has gone by that name ever since.

Over the next several months, Della worked at a number of bars and nightclubs. She even worked at a bowling alley. She added some humor to her routine, impressing listeners with her wit as well as her singing. They got to know the young performer and she became the talk of the town. Unfortunately, not all of the talk was positive. For most of her life, Della had been a gospel singer and only performed in churches. According to some churchgoers, a "good Christian" didn't work in bars and nightclubs. Della found herself existing in two worlds: spiritual and secular. She fit in well in both places. She had good friends in both places. She was successful in both places. Della's closest friends, both in church and in the nightclubs, understood and supported her. Even so, Della became the center of criticism by some church people who felt she should not be involved in "the devil's music." Some church boards even reprimanded her for singing secular music in "those" places.

Music was going through many transitions in the 1950s, so Della's difficulties were not unusual. People spoke out about the emerging "dangers" of the newest sensation: rock-n-roll music. Some of the most popular singers, such as Elvis Presley, were even banned in some communities. Because of the rapid growth of the recording industry and people's improved economic situations, music was one of the most important recreations of the time. All over the nation, teenagers were listening to the radio, dancing, and buying records. Older adults who had lived through the Great Depression found the music scene a bit frightening. Reese understood all of this. She also understood that she had a unique talent and needed to decide where her future was.

Della turned to two of the people she respected most: Reverend Rundless and his wife Earnestine. As a single woman, Della explained that she could not make a living singing only gospel music. She wasn't sure she could make much more money by singing in the clubs. The couple listened and then gave Della the best advice they had to offer: to follow her heart and to remember that just because she worked in places where people made some bad choices did not mean she had to become like those people. She could be "in their world" but not be "of their world." That made sense to Della.

Soon after talking with the Rundlesses, Della discovered that she had been nominated as Detroit's favorite local singer as a result of a contest sponsored by an area newspaper and beverage company. People mailed in the ballots that appeared in the newspaper. A crowd favorite because of her good nature and tremendous talent, Della easily won the honor. Her prize included a makeover, some makeup, a gown, and the chance to perform for a week at the Flame Showbar nightclub. Some of the best black singers performed there. This was the big time for a city like Detroit. Della earned 85 dollars for the week's performance. She was pleasantly surprised when they asked her to perform for another eighteen weeks. Never before had she earned so much money doing what she loved most. Finally, Della believed that she really could sing for a living.

Della Reese was the opening act for all the big-name performers who came to the Flame. Just as she had done with Mahalia Jackson, Della listened and learned. She admired and respected the people she got to know at the Flame, including singers Sammy Davis Jr., Billy Eckstine, Ella Fitzgerald, Sarah Vaughan, Dinah Washington, and Carmen McRae.

Della won the honor of Detroit's favorite local singer in a contest sponsored by an area newspaper and beverage company. Her prize was a makeover, a gown, and chance to perform at the Flame Showbar as the opening act for some of the top entertainers of the day. She listened to, and learned from, every single performer.

The lesson that had begun with Mahalia Jackson now continued with these singers. They showed Reese that her goal was not to sing like them, but to sing in her own special way. She learned that in the world of performing, she needed to be strong and confident, but maintain humility and strive for excellence.

Mahalia's lessons kept coming back as Della moved into the secular music world. They worked here just as well. In fact, in some ways they worked even better. In the secular music world, there was no room for imitation. Audiences wanted fresh, new styles. Performers who tried to sound like someone else were often ridiculed for trying to sing someone else's songs. Della, who could sing so many kinds of music—blues, jazz, gospel, swing, and pop—found and displayed her own style in each one. She also learned about the importance of having good makeup and beautiful costumes. That was another difference between secular and church performing. Della practiced her entrances and exits, learning to move gracefully despite some tight-fitting costumes. Della seldom smiled, self-conscious about her imperfect teeth. The owner of one of the clubs paid to have her teeth fixed so she would share her gorgeous smile with the public. It worked! Della's smile is still one of her hallmarks.

One evening while performing at the Flame, Della noticed a new man sitting up front. He was being treated as if he were a very important person. She asked some of the other performers who the fuss was all about. They told her the VIP was Daddy Braggs, one of the top black promoters in the Michigan club scene. Della performed as usual, and the crowd loved her. Afterward, she was walking toward her dressing room in the basement when Daddy Braggs approached her. He told her, "You're good. You oughta be a star." Della smiled and answered, "I am." Daddy Braggs laughed loudly, clearly enjoying her confidence. Then he offered her 100 dollars to "buy a new dress." Della told him "no thanks." Braggs had probably never heard that from an up-and-coming star. Fortunately, Daddy Braggs was not offended. Instead, he hired Della to perform at Paradise, one of only two exclusive black resorts.

The summer of 1951 was exciting. Della loved the upscale resort and the attention Daddy Braggs gave to the shows he sponsored. Unlike the basic nightclub scene she had been working in, the resort gig was complete with costume designers, choreographers, the best lighting and sound systems, and a full orchestra. Della and Daddy Braggs became good friends. He encouraged her work as a performer. When the summer was over, she moved on to Chicago to continue singing. This time the gig was at a very popular black-owned nightclub. Daddy Braggs kept track of how she was doing, and he invited her to return to Paradise in the summer of 1952, as the star act. Some of the songs she sang night after night at the Paradise included "One for My Baby," "There Will Never Be Another You," and "Headin' Home." She later recorded some of these songs.

During Della's second summer at Paradise, Tony Vance, the owner of a record company in Chicago, was in the audience. He listened with interest to this exciting new talent. He told Della he wanted her to come to Chicago to make a record. There was no doubt that her career was now on the fast track. Throughout her young career, Della often seemed to be at the right place at the right time. Thrilled at the chance to record, Della agreed. She recorded four songs with Duke Ellington's band. The records were played in the Chicago/Detroit area. Della had many job offers as a result of getting to be so well known.

Traveling from town to town and living out of a suitcase, Della soon realized that she had no time to focus on the business side of her career. It was time to find a manager. A manager is someone who works hard on behalf of performers, finding them better and better jobs. They also set up meetings with important people in the industry. The most important job of a manager is to get a singer the best recording contract he or she can get. In 1953, Della signed with

New York manager Lee Magid. He continued in that role for the next 22 years.

Della traveled often to New York. Many singers who started in the Midwest went to New York because it was the center of live entertainment in the 1950s. Even in the North, some of the most upscale hotels would not allow blacks to stay there. As a result, many of the black performers got to know each other because they had to stay at a limited number of places. Della did not see this as an injustice as much as she chose to see it as an opportunity. Eventually she got to sing with the very well-known Erskine Hawkins Band. She also went on the road to sing backup for Nat "King" Cole, probably the most well-known and best-loved black singer of his time. "King" Cole was one of the few performers who made Della so nervous that she could barely speak when he was around, so great was her admiration of him, personally and professionally. They were welcomed in clubs all over New York. It was one of the greatest years in Della's rising career.

In 1954, Della made her first record with Jubilee Records. She was just 23 years old. Jubilee was one of the biggest black recording companies in the country. The song, "In the Still of the Night," sold more than 500,000 copies, a remarkable achievement for a black singer in the 1950s. When a black singer made a record that was popular, it was customary for whites in the industry to record the same song using one of the most popular singers of the time. This was called "covering" a song. Society was still very segregated, so the white version of the song usually sold more than the black one. Nevertheless, both black and white listeners responded to Della's record and she had a best seller her first time out. Della's next record was "And That Reminds Me," which she recorded in 1957. Almost immediately, the song was "covered" by Elvis Presley, Kay Starr, and Pat Boone, three of the top singers in the white music industry. It didn't

Della earned her first gold record in 1957 with "And That Reminds Me," which sold almost one million copies. It landed at number 12 on the Top 40s chart, and the title track was covered by Elvis Presley, Kay Starr, and Pat Boone.

matter. "And That Reminds Me" sold almost one million copies, earning Della her first gold record. It landed at number 12 on the Top 40s chart, an indicator of the most popular songs of the day, black and white. Della was on top of the world. She was even happier when her first royalty check arrived.

Artists (including singers, writers, illustrators) earn royalties on their work. This is a percentage of the total sales of whatever the product is. For every one of her records that sold, Della would earn money. Periodically, a check was issued to her for the total amount of her royalties for what had been sold up to that time. Della's first royalty check from Jubilee Records was for $5,656.23. It was more money than she had ever seen. She cashed the check and went out shopping. Her first purchase was 12 pairs of shoes! Walking joyfully in them, she had no idea that everything would change the very next day. Someone from Jubilee Records called her to tell her that she owed the company about $18,000 in expenses. Of course, she did not have that kind of money and she had no idea that she owed them anything. She demanded to look at their accounting books. Seeing some confusing things in the books, she had Lee Magid go to the offices and look at them, too. He also thought that the numbers were questionable.

The two asked to see the president of Jubilee, Jerry Blaine. Della had seen him in the building just a few minutes earlier, but she was told that he was not in. Knowing that she was being lied to and cheated, Della forced her way into Blaine's office. She screamed and yelled at him, letting him know just how bad his company was. Of course, Della had no way of knowing that Blaine had a heart condition. She told him, "If you don't give me all of my money, God will strike you dead right here and now." She ranted for a few more minutes, and suddenly Blaine had a heart attack right then and there. Della felt so bad, she started praying out loud, asking God not to let him die. He very nearly did. Eventually Blaine recovered, but Della's career at Jubilee was over. With her new shoes it was time to go shopping for a new recording company.

6

THE BIG TIME

DELLA REESE MAY have had a gold record, but she never saw another penny of royalties from it. Most singers can expect to earn money from a hit like "And That Reminds Me" for many years. Royalties are paid whenever the record is sold or whenever it is played on the radio. Even though Della did not earn what she could have from this record, it did its magic for her career in other ways. It was because of that song that she was asked to appear on *The Ed Sullivan Show*. It was one of the most popular TV shows in the country.

Della's television career began on Ed Sullivan's stage. Sullivan's wife loved "And That Reminds Me." In fact, Della soon found out that the Sullivans considered it their "love song." The *Ed Sullivan Show* was the most-watched television program on Sunday evenings. Sullivan hosted the entertainment variety show, introducing many kinds of talents that included singers, musicians, comedians, and actors. Some of the more unusual performances were animal acts, mimes, and puppets.

Della knew an appearance on the show was a monumental opportunity. The entire country would not only hear her voice but would also see her perform. The first time Della appeared, she gladly sang "And That Reminds Me." The young black singer was seen and heard in living rooms across the country. On

Her successful, live show in clubs all over the country led to television appearances on variety shows in the late 1950s. The master of ceremonies of one of the shows, Ed Sullivan, became a good friend of Della, along with his wife. These two people later insisted Della be treated well during a time when blacks were not considered the equals of whites.

Sullivan's show, race was not an issue. In fact, Ed Sullivan was responsible for opening doors for many black and Hispanic performers. Sullivan and Della grew to be good friends. He had her appear on the show 18 times that year, each time requesting that she sing the same song, "And That Reminds Me." Della was always happy to do so.

The public took notice of this young talent. The top three entertainment newspapers, *Variety*, *Billboard*, and *Cashbox*, voted Della "Most Promising Young Singer" of 1957. Being chosen by all three put Della's name before all of the important people in the business. She was surprised and very pleased with the honor.

With her ever-increasing popularity, Della was constantly on the road, going from one appearance to another. She was living out of her suitcase, often driving great distances. All the traveling was becoming exhausting. She was also doing more and more work in New York. Her home base was still Detroit, where her closest friends and family lived. Della knew that she needed to move to New York. It was time to make a home somewhere. Her friends were very sad, but they understood and they supported her decision. This time, Della was really leaving home.

The transition for Della was made easier because she already had made so many friends in New York. Wherever she went, people liked her. Word of mouth about her talent and her personality opened opportunities for her to perform in the best places. One of the hottest places to sing was a nightclub in Harlem (*the* place to be in those days) called the Baby Grand. Soon after moving to New York, she was invited to sing there. One of the warmest, funniest men in show business, Nipsy Russell, was the emcee at the Baby Grand. He and Della became friends right away.

One evening while Della was performing at the Grand, a gentleman named Bobby Shiffman came to

see her. He was the owner of an even bigger place, the Apollo Theater, which was next door to the Grand. Shiffman had been following Della's career for a while and knew how well she was doing. He asked her to perform at his club. Della knew that an opportunity to sing at the Apollo was huge, and would lead to even more performance opportunities in cities like Washington, DC, and Baltimore, Maryland. She was right. Soon, Della was traveling to those towns, too, working with such legends as Cab Calloway and

Performing at the Apollo Theater in New York City took Della and her career away from family and friends in Detroit. She knew the move was a necessary one; it also placed her even closer to more work in Baltimore and Washington, DC. Her professional life was in full swing, but why did she feel so empty inside?

George Kirby, two of the greatest black performers of that era. All of this had happened in only one month. Della had no more doubts about making it in show business. She knew she had arrived.

The following year, Della met a young accountant named Leroy Gray. After a short courtship, the two decided to get married. They traveled back to Chicago to have the ceremony. Friend and fellow singer Johnny Mathis sang at their wedding. Unfortunately there was trouble in the marriage almost right away. Before they married, Della did not know that Leroy had strong opinions about white people. He didn't like Della having a white man managing her career. No matter how much Della defended Magid, her new husband didn't like it. Even worse, Della discovered that Leroy was an atheist, someone who did not believe in God. He explained that he couldn't believe in God because of how his aunt had treated him as a child. She had beaten him "in the name of God." Della understood, but prayed that her husband would change. She knew from her previous marriage that she could not change this man herself. It would be up to God. She decided to let him handle the situation, determined to be patient and loving. A short time later, they found out that Leroy's previous marriage had not been legally ended. He was still married to his first wife. Knowing that their differences were too great, they agreed to annul their marriage. An annulment says that the marriage never really existed because of legal issues. The relationship ended.

With another failed marriage, Della wondered if she would ever find the husband God had waiting for her. She decided to go home to Detroit for a while. She got a gig at the Flame, going back to a place comfortable and familiar. One night her father came to see her perform. Richard had never seen his daughter sing. Della was delighted see his face in the audience. Afterward, they had their picture taken, and she could see by his beaming smile that he was proud of her. It was a very special night. Just a year later, Richard Early passed away while Della was in New York.

Della had been sending her father money for years, but had a hunch he didn't spend it. She was right. He had saved every penny. Richard Early had written a letter to his only daughter to be read after his death. In it, he told her that he wished he had lived his life differently. He also told Della that her aunt would tell her where everything was. "Everything" turned out to be all the money she had been sending. There it was, under the carpet. Richard wanted his daughter to have it, to spend on herself. She was sad to lose her father, but was comforted by knowing that he was now in heaven with Nellie, his only true love.

While she was in Detroit for her father's funeral, Della found out that her sister-in-law Delores, R.D.'s wife, was very ill and pregnant with their sixth child. The family knew that R.D. and Delores could not afford—on any level—to have another child. Della offered to take the child and raise it as her own. At first, R.D. and Delores agreed. However, once the little girl arrived on November 29, 1959, Delores changed her mind. She did not want to give up her child, who she named Deloreese. Della understood and went back to New York to continue her career.

Della's recording career took off when she began to make records for RCA, one of the biggest labels in the country. She had another gold record, "Don't You Know," her very first record with RCA. The song had been written just for her and was based on an aria (opera song) from Puccini's *La Boheme*. The song, which was to be her biggest hit, earned Della a Grammy nomination for best female vocalist that year.

As a result, Della was invited to sing at the very best clubs throughout New York, not just those in

Harlem. These included the Copacabana, the Coconut Grove, and the Fairmont. By 1961, Della had achieved nearly all of her goals. She was as successful as she had ever dreamed of being. But something was missing. She was very lonely. Della tried filling her loneliness by going to lots and lots of parties. It didn't change how she felt. Yet she knew that this ache in her heart was there for a reason. Della's faith told her that she was being prepared for something.

One night during the winter of 1962, Della was scheduled to perform in Chicago. As she was rehearsing for the evening set, R.D. and Delores walked in with two-year-old Deloreese. They had decided that Della should raise the little girl as her own. Della was cautious, reminding them that they had changed their minds before. She told them that there would be no going back on this deal. It would break Della's heart to have to give up the child once she had her. She then reminded R.D. of the times his own father had come to take him back. R.D. and Delores promised that they would not change their minds. Even as they talked, little Deloreese snuggled up to Della, already feeling at home with her new mother.

After R.D. and Delores left, Della kept the child with her. After the show that night, she wrapped the little girl in her big chinchilla fur coat and carried her back to the hotel room. The next day they flew home to New York. The emptiness Della had felt was finally filled. This child was just what she needed and God had provided, as Della knew he would.

Deloreese called Della "mama" from the first day. Their bond was as real as any between a mother and daughter, and it remains so to this day. For the next four years, the two were inseparable. Wherever Della went, little Deloreese was there, too. At three and one-half years old, Deloreese decided that she wanted to change her name. She told her mother that she wanted her own name. Della asked her what name

she would like. Without hesitation, the little girl answered, "Dumpsey." No one knows where that name came from, but "Dumpsey" was happy to have her own name at last.

The mother-and-daughter duo did not travel only in the United States. Della's popularity was growing worldwide. They traveled to England, Australia, Italy, Brazil, and other countries. Della was well received wherever she went, deluged with flowers and standing ovations. By 1962 she wanted to broaden her act to include the music that was closest to her heart—gospel. No one else was performing gospel music in secular settings like nightclubs. The only place gospel

In 1962, Della adopted her niece, later self-named Dumpsey. Dumpsey brought meaning to Della's life and gave her new understanding of a fulfilling love. More records and live shows at the best theaters in the cities, black or white, granted her higher status in the entertainment industry. She was then asked to be guest host of "The Tonight Show Starring Johnny Carson;" she is pictured here with Ed McMahon.

could be found was in churches. Della Reese was about to change that.

Della invited her Meditation Singers to join her at the Copacabana in New York. Her Detroit friends were thrilled to come and sing with her again. Crossing their fingers, they performed before the secular crowd. The audience loved it. For some reason, Della knew she had to take this act to Las Vegas. This was probably the last city in America where people would expect to hear gospel music. Perhaps that was why Della chose it in the first place.

When church leaders heard about Della's plans, they were outraged. Church music didn't belong in "Sin City," the gambling mecca of America. They weren't alone in their opinion. The secular promoters in Las Vegas didn't think anyone would come to hear that sort of music either. Somehow though, Della got her chance. Her act, called "Portrait of Della Reese," followed the styles of her career—from gospel to blues to jazz to pop music. The show was a hit. In fact, it was so popular that RCA decided to record the show and release it as an album. It was also filmed for TV. Night after night, Della and her singers played to sold-out houses.

Las Vegas was a good performing town for Della. She was loved and appreciated for her talent. Unfortunately, Vegas was also still very segregated in its treatment of entertainers. While Della could perform at the nightclubs and hotels, she could not go into the casinos or eat or stay at the hotels because she was black. Black performers had to stay across town at a place called the Dust Bowl.

Not everyone in Las Vegas agreed with this treatment. Ed Sullivan, whose show was aired from this city, did not have a racist bone in his body. One evening Della ordered a cheeseburger from room service to be delivered backstage. She had not eaten all day and knew she needed some nourishment before performing that evening. She waited and waited, but no food ever arrived. Sullivan happened to be walking by as he heard someone explain that Della could not be served in this establishment. He was appalled to find that she was being treated like this. He called room service himself and Della got her cheeseburger. After that, Mr. Sullivan and his wife took Della with them to the best restaurants in Vegas. Della owed him much for helping her through those difficult times.

For the next nine years, Della played in Las Vegas, usually 26 weeks a year. She met some entertainment greats, like Sammy Davis Jr., Sarah Vaughan, and "Ol' Blue Eyes" himself, Frank Sinatra. During those years, she also recorded more hits, including "Bill Bailey," "It Was a Very Good Year," and "Sunny." These years were lonelier because she had to put Dumpsey in school while she was on the road. Della tells people that her phone bill was as big as the national budget during that time. Being out West so much of the year, Della knew it was time to buy a home in Los Angeles. She could spend more time with Dumpsey because LA was only a 45-minute flight from Las Vegas. She found a nice house for the two of them and hired a housekeeper/nanny named Miss Molly Toliver. Miss Molly reminded Della of Nellie, and she remained with Della and Dumpsey for 25 years.

In the mid-1960s Della was making more appearances on television. She loved this part of her career. Up until this time, she had only been asked to sing on TV programs. That was how it was for blacks in the 1960s. However, when she appeared on the *Merv Griffin Show*, a popular variety program of the time, he invited her to come "sit on the couch." That was an invitation to be interviewed. Della was warm and funny, and was a great interviewee. She was asked often to come back on the show. There were other popular variety shows, too. Hosts included Mike Douglas, Jackie Gleason, Steve Allen, and Johnny Carson. Some were daytime shows; some were nighttime. Most variety shows were filmed before a live audience and included a combination of singing, comedy, interviews, animal acts, and others. *The Tonight Show,* which in those days was hosted by Johnny Carson, was the first to ask a black performer to guest-host when Mr. Carson could not appear. That black performer was Della Reese.

Della was becoming a household name on television. Still, she had never had a chance to *act,* rather than sing or talk. In 1968 she finally got her chance. She made a guest appearance on the very popular TV drama *The Mod Squad.* After that, other guest shots came along. Della also got to be a "square" on the game show *Hollywood Squares.* Her vivacious personality and wonderful wit made her a favorite "*Squares*" celebrity.

The breakthrough year was 1969. Producer Woody Fraser called Della and asked her the question she had been waiting to hear: "Would you like to do your own TV show?" Della knew that Fraser was a good producer. He had produced *The Mike Douglas Show.* She of course said, "Yes!" One month later, Fraser showed Della his plans for the new show, simply called *Della.* Two weeks later they aired the first show.

Della Reese was the first black woman in television history to host her own program. It appeared five nights a week and was seen in most major northern cities and parts of the South. The show, like most variety shows, included many segments— interviews, music, cooking spots—and had the best of the best musicians, singers, and guests. It was similar to such modern shows as *Regis and Kelly* and *The Tonight Show with Jay Leno.* Della's list of celebrity guests included actor Vincent Price and singers Bobby Darin, Tony Bennett, Kenny Rogers, and Ethel Waters (Della's gospel-singing idol). *Della* had strong ratings, and stayed on the air for two years.

Robert King on the "Della" show that ran from 1969 to 1971, five nights a week. Della was the first woman in the history of television to have her own show, and her personality shone in interviews with other singers and actors. The television experience was a valuable one, but the program was unfortunately cancelled after only two seasons.

Della and Dumpsey were doing well, too. The house they lived in, however, was becoming a problem. Because it was easily accessible, people kept dropping by whenever they felt like it. This bothered Della because she was trying to raise Dumpsey as normally as possible and wanted some privacy for herself and her daughter. Dumpsey had also become a good swimmer and Della wanted her to have her own pool. With her career in good shape, Della felt she could finally buy the house of her dreams. She called a realtor and got ready to "move up" to Bel Air, California.

7

TRAUMA AND
TURNING POINT

Ray Charles and Della sing a duet. Ray's singing and music career has been even more successful and long-lived than Della's. Growing up poor in Albany, Georgia, Ray started losing his sight at the age of 4 and was completely blind by 7. The two have severe physical trauma in common. Della almost lost her life in an accident at her home in 1970. Both are examples of triumph overcoming tragedy, of light transcending darkness.

NOT LONG AFTER moving into her new home on Bel Air Road, Della and her 10-year-old adopted daughter Dumpsey decided to go for a swim. Finally they had their own swimming pool, and they were going to enjoy it. Della opened the sliding glass door that separated the pool from the interior of the house. Soon after, Dumpsey followed, closing the door behind her. Mother and daughter swam, laughed, and soaked in the warmth of the water. But Della knew the air was going to feel cool once they got out. She decided to go into the house for some towels for the two of them while Dumpsey waited in the pool.

The air was cold against Della's wet skin. Shivering slightly, she rushed toward the door, thinking it was still open. Instead, she walked right into the glass and heard a great shattering sound. The center of the door had broken into thousands of pieces and fell to the ground. Jagged shards remained at the top and bottom of the frame. Della's forward movement had been suddenly stopped and she lost her balance. Falling forward, Della landed on the sharp broken pieces of glass. She felt the glass cut into her stomach. Time after time she tried to stand up, but kept slipping down again. Each time the glass cut deeper into her abdomen.

"I've been through the valley of the shadow of

death," says Della. "I walked through that glass. My brain exploded." Broken glass was all around her, cutting her hands, legs, and feet. Above her, a large razor-sharp section began to loosen. Della refers to what happened next as one of her "angel" moments. She couldn't get up. Over and over she tried. Still something told her she had to get up *now*. Then something miraculous happened. Della says she actually felt her mother's presence take hold of her and lift her from the doorway. Nellie had died in 1949, but Della says she knew it was her, "because it was her smell, her smell only, that wonderful-smelling mixture of Ponds cold cream, vanilla, and spices. As she lifted me and told me to sit down, that scent overwhelmed me," says Della.

By this time, Dumpsey had run into the house for towels. Aided by the memory of Nellie's days healing and mending people's wounds, Della told her daughter what to do. Dumpsey used one towel to form a tourniquet on her mother's bleeding leg to slow down the loss of blood.

Next Dumpsey ran to a neighbor's house for help. This neighbor happened to be a surgeon, Dr. Harvey Cantor. When he arrived, he was shocked to see how badly Della had been cut. He called for an ambulance and actually held Della's body together with his hands as they sped to the UCLA Medical Center.

When Della arrived at the hospital, doctors would not begin to work on her until an adult family member signed her in. Ten-year-old Dumpsey was the only one with her. Precious minutes were slipping by as the doctors waited. Somehow Della heard them. And she got mad. She opened her eyes and said clearly, "Give me the papers. I'll sign them myself." The doctors were stunned. They thought she was unconscious. Given the papers, Della quickly signed them and then passed out again.

Della had lost about seven pints of blood, an astounding amount, since the human body usually

holds only about eight or nine pints. Somehow Della held on. She considers her recovery a miracle. Even so, doctors were concerned that the one leg that had been cut so badly might not work properly again. They put a cast on it and told Della that she might have to live without the use of that leg. They kept her leg up in the air by attaching it to a sling that was anchored to the ceiling. In great pain because of the 1,000 stitches in her body, Della could not move into any comfortable position. Through all the trauma and talk of death, Della held onto her belief that she would be all right. But her true turning point was just around the corner.

Della was a very successful singer and actress. She had already sold millions of records as a gospel, jazz, and blues singer. Della's easy, welcoming ways made her a favorite wherever she went. She began to make appearances on television in the 1950s and 1960s, a time when few African Americans had success on TV. By 1970, she even had her own TV

Della was wounded badly when she crashed through the sliding glass door in her home. She was rushed to the UCLA Medical Center, having lost nearly seven pints of blood and requiring close to 1,000 stitches. Della considers it a miracle that she survived the accident.

Della with daughter Dumpsey in Los Angeles, 2001. After her accident in 1970, at a high point of her career, Della had a spiritual awakening. She realized all of the awards, clothes, and money in the world could not give her the same satisfaction as her daughter, others of her family, God, and living life fully. She sang about this revelation in "I Am Proud to Praise the Lord" in her first concert after recovering from her accident.

show, *Della.* Wealthy, successful, admired, Della was at the top of her world. But it took a life-threatening accident to show her that success was small compared to what really mattered.

When Della was sent home from the hospital, her leg was still in a cast and still had to be elevated, hanging from the ceiling as it had in the hospital. Some of her closest friends, the Sayles family, came to stay with her, and take care of Della while she recovered. These four—Marie Sayles, her husband, her son, and their three-year-old daughter Della Marie—made Della's meals, took care of her house and yard, and tended to her every need. Della appreciated the sacrifice these friends had made for her. Still, day after day of not being able to take care of herself made Della a little frustrated. Whenever she needed something, Della rang a little bell. Soon someone would come and bring her water, help her to the bathroom, or help her with another request.

One very hot day, Della was thirsty. She desperately needed a glass of water. So she rang her bell. She waited. No one came. So she rang the bell again. Then louder. Finally, she rang the bell so hard that it broke. Still no one came. Della looked around, hoping to get an idea of how she could get up and take care of her thirst. As she scanned the bedroom, she looked at her open jewelry box across the way. From her bed, Della could see a treasure chest of diamonds, pearls, gold and silver pieces, bracelets, earrings, and pins. Then she looked over at her closet where her mink coats hung like expensive trophies. All of these great possessions were just out of reach. And none of them could do a thing to help her with a need as basic as giving her water to drink.

That moment changed Della Reese. Without even realizing how her life's direction had changed, a shift had taken place within her. All these riches had been evidence of her success. She had a beautiful new home on a mountaintop and the best jewelry and clothing money could buy. Things had become too important to her. But now, simply needing that glass of water helped Della straighten out her thinking. Since that day she has kept her focus on the important things: family, God, and living life fully.

Just a few minutes after Della had come to this decision, little three-year-old Della Marie came into the bedroom. The tiny messenger then went outside to tell her parents that Della needed them inside. "My angels came to my side quickly," recalls Della with a smile.

After only one month of physical therapy, Della Reese was back on her feet again. She walked everywhere, grateful that she had the full use of her legs. While she had been bedridden, Della wrote some songs. One of them, "I'm Proud to Praise the Lord," was included in her first performance after the accident. She told the audience at the Century Plaza Hotel in Los Angeles all about her accident and the "angels" who helped her along the way. Reliving the experience, Della shared her feelings and discoveries with everyone there. No doubt about it—Della was back. And her angels were right there with her, too.

8

TOUGH YEARS AND
FALLEN ANGELS

✿

DELLA'S RECOVERY FROM the accident was nothing short of miraculous. She went back to her show and made the adjustments she had to make so "the show could go on." Wigs covered the cuts on her scalp and forehead, makeup hid her scars, and set changes allowed Della to sit more. The show was doing well, but the sponsors kept finding fault. They criticized Della's hair, her clothes, everything but the show itself. Still, everyone was shocked when the announcement came that the show had been cancelled. Della knew it was about race. Southern stations were slow to pick up a program with a black host. Indignant, Della demanded a reason for the cancellation.

"Because your gums are blue," she was told. Blue? Of course they were blue. Many African Americans have blue gums. There was no doubt in Della's mind that she was being cast off because of her race. She knew how to think about racist people. Her mother had taught her that anyone who judges another purely on a racial basis was ignorant. Della learned early in her life to forgive and just move on. That is exactly what she did. Not missing a beat, she let the music world know that she was available to work again. That meant going back on the road.

She traveled to Chicago, one of her favorite places to perform. Watching the new, up-and-coming

A photo of Della in 1971, the year her show was cancelled. The reason? 'Because her gums were blue.' Della's reaction to this prejudice was to forgive, acknowledge the reason was ignorant, and move on. A harder blow were two "fallen angels," the lawyer and accountant who stole money from her. She had to relearn how to trust such professionals.

black performers helped Della see just how far she had come. She was more relaxed about her career than she had been the last time she worked the clubs. Watching these young people, she remembered how each opportunity became the focus of her life, as if it were the very one that would push her to greater heights. Now she saw things through more mature eyes, understanding that life, even work, was a process that moved from one thing to the next. Della was at peace with her life, knowing it was enough to be the mother of Dumpsey and a daughter of God.

In many ways, the 1970s were a slow time for Della Reese. She still recorded songs and albums, moving from RCA to ABC and then to another recording company. One highlight was a 1972 disco hit called "If It Feels Good Do It," a kind of motto for the decade. Otherwise, her records were not selling well at all. But Della wasn't worried. By this time, she was more interested in building her acting career. One downside to her decision was the loss of her manager, Lee Magid. He managed singers and musicians, and he felt he could not adequately help Della with her acting career. Sadly, after 22 years together, they parted.

Agents in Los Angeles were busy trying to find acting jobs for Della. While she waited for good news from them, she got bad news about her financial situation. One of her attorneys in LA, a man she had trusted for more than ten years, had stolen money from her. Della had given him full power of attorney over her affairs. This meant that he could sign any papers for her as if she were signing them herself, even without her knowledge. Della was both angry and heartbroken to discover that he had stolen more than $250,000 from her.

About the same time she learned about her attorney, she found out that one of her accountants had also stolen from her. Della sent money to this man to pay her taxes. Instead he had used it to buy real estate for himself. She might not have learned about this if the IRS had not told her she was almost $500,000 behind in her taxes. The amount stunned her. A friend advised Della to get the best tax attorney she could find before the IRS took her home and all her possessions. The first step was to find the right attorney. Trusting anyone now would be a challenge. She prayed that God would take care of what she could not.

Thankfully, Della found the right person for the job. She met with a highly recommended tax attorney in Los Angeles. She walked in feeling hopeless and weak. After looking over her records, the attorney had good news. The IRS numbers seemed to him to be in error—she could never owe that much money to the government based on her income. On her way out of the attorney's office, Della prayed, telling God that it was all up to him. She was determined to accept God's way in this matter and to be grateful for whatever she had left. Della didn't have to wonder for long how things would turn out. The tax attorney was able to get the taxes due to the IRS down to $100,000. She could handle that. All was well. Again, God had provided.

The agents who were working hard for Della finally had good news, too. She was offered a part on a new TV show called *Flo's Place*. The costar was Ernest Borgnine, a well-known film actor. They filmed the pilots, which are test episodes, to see if there were enough interest to develop a series. Unfortunately, the series never happened, but Della met some important people as a result. Tapes of the episodes were sent to James Komack, the producer of the show *Chico and the Man*. He was looking for an actress to play the female lead role on the show. After he saw the tapes from *Flo's Place*, Komack offered Della the job.

Chico and the Man was one of the first multicultural shows on television. The cast included Jack

Albertson, an elderly white actor, Freddie Prinze, a young Hispanic actor, Scatman Crothers, a comedian, and Della Reese. The sitcom took place in a barrio, or Hispanic neighborhood, of Los Angeles. Jack and Freddie worked in a garage in a Spanish-speaking part of the city. Freddie Prinze was Chico, a happy-go-lucky young man, and Jack Albertson played Ed Brown, the grumpy garage owner. Della played Della Rogers, the owner of the local diner.

The cast and crew of *Chico and the Man* became as close as family. Because the show was filmed in Los Angeles, Della did not have to travel to go to work. She and Dumpsey were able to spend more time together. The show was an immediate hit. The talent of the cast captivated the viewing audience. Prinze, a young, pop idol, captured the hearts and imaginations of teenage girls all over the country. Remembering him, Della tells people that she truly loved working with such an energetic and loving person. But Freddie Prinze died of a self-inflicted gunshot wound in 1977, when his young son, Freddie Jr., was only 10 months old. Everyone on the show was devastated by the news.

Chico and the Man went on, despite Freddie's tragic death. The writers wove a story line that had Chico returning home to Mexico. Another young actor was introduced as a new character, but after Prinze's death the show was never the same. Top-name performers like Sammy Davis Jr. and Shelley Winters made guest appearances. *Chico and the Man* survived four seasons before being canceled. These years were some of Della's best in television. All three of the men Della worked with on the show—Jack Albertson, Scatman Crothers, and Freddie Prinze—are now gone. She misses them, but believes they are part of the team watching over her from heaven.

With no other TV shows on the horizon, Della set out again for the singing circuit. This time "back on the road" was really "sailing the seas" for her. She

Della and Freddie Prinze on "Chico and the Man." The show ended a year after Freddie shot himself at a party. 'A prank gone bad' was Della's interpretation of his apparent suicide. Such tragedies and their effect on others would be a topic frequently explored on her best-known show, "Touched By An Angel."

was booked to perform on cruise ships that sailed to the Caribbean, Bermuda, Rio de Janeiro, and Alaska. It was a restful time for her, relaxing and being pampered on the luxury liners.

In 1978 Della was contacted by one of the leading advertising agencies in the country to see if she might be interested in being the spokesperson for a Borden Foods product. Just like Tiger Woods does commercial endorsements for Nike today, manufacturers liked to have celebrities do commercials for their products back then, too. Companies like having recognizable people representing their products, and celebrities get to keep their faces in the public view. Della had already been a spokesperson for Kraft Foods, so she was glad to have this opportunity.

The executives of this new ad agency wanted Della because she appealed to so many different races. One of the agency's executives, Franklin Lett, was not sure she was the right choice, however. He was unfamiliar with Della and her work. Still, he agreed that he should meet with her before making a decision. Franklin's office was in Chicago, so he didn't meet with Della until she had a gig there. He attended one of her shows and was impressed by her genial nature and style. They met at the Ritz Carlton Hotel to talk about the job. Still a bit cautious because of her previous experiences with "professionals" like the attorney and accountant, Della watched him closely. Soon, though, she was impressed with his business savvy and positive nature. The meeting went very well, and she expected she soon would have good news about the job.

Months went by. Franklin called from time to time, always apologizing about how slowly things were progressing. They chatted casually and became good friends over the phone. As it turned out, they both had grown up in Detroit and had even been in Chicago at the same times. Up until now, their paths had never crossed. Della had been very busy with her career and with raising her daughter. She was not looking for another husband. Still as the months went by, their calls became more personal and even loving. She began to wonder, is this the one God has chosen for me?

In 1979 the two met frequently. A true love was developing between them. Knowing that God had set this all up, Della tried to be patient while Franklin came to terms with this new woman in his life. He had gone through a difficult divorce and was not eager to marry again soon. Della just kept loving and caring for him, baking him his favorite pies and delivering them to him in person. All the while she kept wondering if Franklin Lett was the man she was meant to spend her life with.

That spring, Della was performing in Chicago in their rendition of *Same Time, Next Year*. For six weeks she was in Franklin's town. They enjoyed each other's company immensely. Despite their wonderful times together, Della again felt that something else was missing. Her hair and makeup man for the show kept telling Della about someone named Johnnie, about how much Della reminded him of her. As it turned out, Johnnie was his minister, Mrs. Johnnie Coleman. Della was invited to visit one of her services at Christ Universal Temple on the south side of Chicago. Almost immediately, the emptiness Della had been feeling disappeared. A deeply spiritual woman, Della had been away from good Bible teaching for too long. Della also liked Johnnie right away. What's more, this church turned out to be Franklin's church, too. During those weeks while Della was in Chicago, she and Franklin attended together. Della was asked to sing and to speak, and she felt right at home doing both.

The six weeks went by quickly, and the final day of the show was also Della's birthday, July 6, 1979. The sadness Della felt about leaving was noticeable, and the cast planned a big party to celebrate Della's birthday and the success of the show. Before the party, Della and Franklin knew they needed to decide what their next step together would be. Though his roots and his children were in Chicago, Franklin decided he wanted to come to Los Angeles so he could be with Della. The party was a celebration of a wonderful beginning for Franklin and Della, too.

Franklin needed to find work or start a business once he arrived in LA. Della had the perfect solution: he would become her manager. His business knowledge, advertising background, and fine character made him the perfect man for the job. He eventually agreed. Della kept waiting for him to ask her to marry him, but the question never seemed to come. They visited family in Detroit in 1980, and while they were there, Della explained that she couldn't wait forever. "Life could end at any moment, and we're messing around and wasting it," she told him.

After a nice visit with both sides of the family, Della and Franklin returned to California. Della was scheduled to appear on *The Tonight Show*, which was being guest-hosted by a good friend, Richard Dawson (the first host of *Family Feud*). Della selected the song "Pieces of Dreams" to sing in her spot on the show. She took center stage, let the music begin, and sang about six words. Suddenly something went horribly wrong. She hit "the worst note of her life" and began to convulse, falling to the floor in a dead faint. A nurse in the audience rushed to the stage, and someone called for an ambulance. Franklin, who had gone to the taping with Della, rode to the hospital with her.

Because she was overweight, the doctors thought she was having an episode related to high blood pressure. Her vital statistics, which include temperature, blood pressure, and pulse, were all normal. They moved her to a hospital closer to her home, where her doctor practiced. Della had never listed her mother's cause of death in her own medical records. She should have, because she was experiencing the same thing Nellie had so many years before: an aneurysm in her brain. This was a life-threatening situation, and the doctors told Franklin that Della might not make it until morning. He never left her side, praying for her throughout the night.

Surprising the doctors, Della woke up the next morning, but was unaware of what had happened or where she was. She was stable enough to be moved to a hospital that had the equipment to diagnose her condition more specifically. After taking several x-rays and other tests, doctors were able to see where the blood vessel had burst. One of the best neurosurgeons in the area was called in to be Della's doctor, but she did not like him. He was very matter-of-fact, often only talking about the negative aspects of her condition. With each passing day Della felt more confused and afraid.

One day after being especially frightened by her doctor's uncertainty about a necessary pre-operation procedure, Della prayed. "Father," she said, "I don't know what decisions to make. I've never heard these words before. I don't understand the language." At that very moment, the door to her room opened and a doctor in green hospital scrubs walked in. When he spoke, his words convinced Della that he was really an angel sent to her by God. "I realize that sometimes patients don't know what decisions to make," he told her. "They've never heard these words before. They don't understand the language. So, if you don't mind, I thought I'd explain the process in everyday language." Della could hardly believe her ears. God had heard her prayer and wasted no time in sending an answer. "All you will have to do is be still," the doctor continued. Suddenly Della's favorite Bible verse sang in her mind: "Be still and know that I am God." This doctor had just the right medicine for his patient—care and information. Della felt at peace and knew she was in good hands.

The next morning the procedure went perfectly, and Della had no pain or fear. Now it was time to get ready for the surgery. Franklin sent all her x-rays and tests to the UCLA Medical Center. The x-rays were so clear, the doctors there felt that any competent surgeon could be successful. Then, they recommended one of the best—Dr. Charles Drake at Ontario's London University Hospital in Canada.

Franklin and Dumpsey accompanied Della to Canada to meet with Dr. Drake. When Della first saw him, she thought he looked like Santa Claus. As it turned out, he was almost as jolly as old Saint Nick. Dr. Drake told the group that the x-rays were good and that it was not an unusual aneurysm to deal with. Della felt great comfort when Dr. Drake told her that God holds his hand when he works on people. She felt so reassured that she told him, "Cut me anywhere you want to cut me." When she was wheeled into the operating room, Della sang "God Is So Wonderful to Me" until the anesthetic took effect. She woke up in the recovery room, still singing the same song she had started.

The day after the surgery, Della awoke in her private room. She searched for a mirror so she could "fix herself up" a bit before Franklin came in. When Della first saw herself, she was shocked. Her head had been completely shaved, and it was covered with a red substance from the surgery. She was afraid that Franklin would hate how she looked. When he walked in and saw her in all her bald glory, he just smiled and commented on how perfectly shaped her head was. Then she became his "sweet little bald-head, red-headed baby." They laughed and laughed about it.

Della was told that she would have to undergo another surgery because the doctor had seen two more aneurysms in her brain. Both were ready to burst at any time. The aneurysms could be corrected, but it had to be done quickly. Ten days later, she had the second surgery. Soon after, Della was released from the hospital. Her recovery was nothing short of miraculous, again. Only ten days after coming home, Della was back to work, doing radio commercials for Campbell's Soup. Della suffered none of the usual problems that might occur with aneurysms and brain surgery. She could walk, talk, think, see, hear, and move just as well as she had before. The only side effects were tiredness and severe itching at the sites of the incisions. In time, both of those problems would remedy themselves.

Della wanted to thank Dr. Drake in a special way. As soon as she was able, she held a concert in London, Ontario, to raise money for the hospital in his name. Dr. Drake, a man who didn't like having much attention, was surprised and touched. Everyone got involved and paid tribute to this great doctor and surgeon. Throughout Della's very frightening and life-threatening experience, Franklin had been her nurse *and* angel. Her earlier words about wasting time were now almost prophetic.

Frank Lett met Della in 1978. 'Is this the man God has chosen for me?' she wondered. Her two previous marriages had not gone well. The couple married in 1983, a few years after Della had two surgeries to repair dangerous burst blood vessels in her brain. Friend and spiritual mentor, Johnnie Coleman, also helped Della through this difficult experience.

9

"GOD LOVES YOU"

❧

IN 1983, FRANKLIN Thomas Lett Jr. married Della Reese. This was the day Della's mother had talked about years earlier, when Della was 17. Her wedding day was one of the happiest of her life, because she knew Franklin was given to her by God. Johnnie Coleman officiated at the ceremony, which was held at the famous Crystal Cathedral in Los Angeles. Della's daughter, Dumpsey, was her mother's maid of honor.

From childhood, Della Reese knew that a higher power was watching over her. Through two brushes with death and many other difficult situations, she depended on her faith in God to help her survive. Since she had met Johnnie Coleman and her staff, Della had been hungry to learn more about applying biblical teachings to everyday life, and as a result she had enrolled in several correspondence courses. She may have waited a long while for Franklin to decide whether he wanted to marry, but she decided she was not going to wait to grow into a better person.

After she learned more about her faith, Della herself began to teach others. Every Tuesday night, eight students gathered for her classes; before long, the group expanded to 75 students, and Della was being asked to officiate at funerals and weddings. It was now clear to her that God wanted her to establish a church for those who needed a new way to find him.

Della may have waited to become a married woman, but she would not wait for her faith to grow. Several trying events in her life convinced her that God had been there all along, helping her through the difficult times. She started the 'UP' church in 1987 in Los Angeles. Through this work, she has touched those who need what God has to offer.

In her prayers, she promised that she would accept whomever he chose to lead her church.

Della never considered that she would be the one who would become the head of her church. No one was available from Johnnie's church in Chicago to establish a new congregation in Los Angeles, and one night Della was awakened suddenly by a strong feeling that God had chosen her to do the job. Through that night, she wrestled with the idea. Finally, she accepted that this was what God wanted, and she began to study even harder to prepare herself for the position. Della knew that if she was to do this, she needed to be ready as quickly as possible. Four years after that night in 1986, Della became a licensed minister.

For three years, Della held church services in her own home, but when some of her neighbors began to complain and others raised issues about zoning in the residential area, the church went "on the road," moving from hotel conference rooms to rented spaces— wherever she could find enough room to hold all the worshipers comfortably. To be recognized as a valid church in the United States, the organization needed to be registered as nonprofit. Della went through the formalities required and chose the title "Understanding Principles for Better Living Church" (UP for short) as the official name of the new church. Until they could find a permanent space, however, members of the congregation continued to meet wherever they could, trusting that God would provide what they needed.

In the meantime, Della continued to take television roles when she found the time. Although most producers wanted to cast her as a mother, neighbor, or singer, Della was hoping something more unusual would come along. Before her role in *Chico and the Man*, Della had had short runs in *Welcome Back Kotter* (1978) and *It Takes Two* (1982), and she enjoyed her role as a judge in the latter program. The critics liked the show's well-written scripts and its popular lead actors—Richard Crenna, Patty Duke Austin, and

Della—in addition to two younger actors who were just beginning their careers: Helen Hunt and Anthony Edwards. After only a few episodes, however, ABC canceled the show. Reese's next role in a TV sitcom was in *Charlie and Company* (1986), a takeoff of the enormously popular *Cosby Show*. The program could not draw similar numbers of viewers, however, and it was canceled in less than a year.

Despite these disappointments, Della was now earning greater recognition among music and TV fans. The year after *Charlie and Company* was canceled, she received a Grammy Award nomination for Best Female Soloist in Gospel Music and an Emmy nomination for her role in the television movie *Nightmare in Badham County*. Then Eddie Murphy, a talented comedian and an actor in his own right, saw some of Della's work and decided to pursue her for a part in his next film, *Harlem Nights* (1989). Starring alongside comics Redd Foxx and Richard Pryor, Della

Eddie Murphy's movie Harlem Nights *starred Richard Pryor and Della. She caught some criticism as a minister for playing a mean character. Acting is only acting, though, and she continued with her work in both roles. Della may be a kind and spiritual person, but she is also a professional.*

In 1991, Della's next television venture was The Royal Family *with former* Sanford and Son *star Redd Foxx playing the role of Al. She enjoyed working on the positive program about a black family who used humor to deal with adversity. How sad it was, therefore, when Redd died during a rehearsal. Here, Della and family members cope with Al's death.*

played a rather immoral character, which drew criticism from some who believed that as a minister she should not have accepted the role.

Eddie Murphy was so impressed with Della's performance, however, that he convinced CBS executives to launch a new sitcom written especially for Reese and Redd Foxx. The program, titled *The Royal Family*, debuted in September 1991. Reese starred as Foxx's wife, the parents in an African-American family that relied on humor to get through tough times. Della was deeply involved in *The Royal Family*, not only because she held a starring role but also because she believed that the show had the potential to positively affect the lives of millions of viewers.

Della Reese loved her costar's sense of humor, but Foxx could be difficult to work with at times and the show's producer seemed to enjoy upsetting his star. One day, following an angry exchange between the producer and Foxx, the actor clutched at a chair as if in great pain. At first the cast and crew thought he was playing a practical joke on everyone, reenacting a scene from the popular sitcom *Sanford and Son* in which his character fakes a heart attack. But this was not an act. Foxx fell to the floor—the victim of an actual attack.

Della rushed to him and held her friend in her arms, praying for him while the cast and crew waited for an ambulance to arrive. Several people, including Foxx's wife, who had been in the studio that day, followed the ambulance as it raced to the hospital. But it was too late. Less than five hours later, doctors told Mrs. Foxx that her husband had died of a heart attack. As she and Della held each other and cried over their loss, however, the program's producers stood nearby discussing what they would do with the program's plot line now that one of the lead characters was gone.

Della had never witnessed such a cold-hearted response to a death. Stunned, she wasted no words telling the executives exactly what she thought of their appalling behavior at the hospital that day. While viewers sent condolences not only to Foxx's wife but also to Della herself, she promised herself that when the show was canceled she would never accept another TV series role.

Still, Della kept watching television, and before long she noticed that CBS seemed to be struggling to measure up to the ratings of its competitors. "CBS, you need me. You really need me," she said one evening, addressing her television set. Then in 1994, she received a call from her agent, asking whether she would like to travel to North Carolina. She was being offered the starring role in a pilot for a new television series, the agent explained.

Della's first reaction was to turn down the

offer immediately. She had had enough of the hard-heartedness she'd experienced in the world of TV programming. But something made her ask for more information about the part. It was a role, her agent said, for a sassy, wise, and loving African-American woman—and by the way, the character was not a human being but an angel. Intrigued by the concept, Della agreed to make the trip to North Carolina, even though she was still convinced that she would ultimately turn down the job.

To her surprise, Reese found that she enjoyed taping the pilot show. One of the reasons was her costar, Roma Downey, who was a delight to work with. Almost immediately the two women developed a close mother-and-daughter relationship. They parted sadly, hoping but not expecting to see one another again. Reese did not believe that such an overtly religious program would ever be accepted by a major network; it simply did not seem like the kind of fare the networks were looking for. She was wrong about at least one network: CBS agreed to run the pilot. It seemed that it really did need Della Reese after all.

Reese not only became the costar of *Touched by an Angel,* but she was also tapped to record the program's theme song. After the first six episodes, CBS's ratings were so promising that it quickly ordered more, and brought in a new producer to fine-tune the show. Martha Williamson became as much of an "angel" to the show's cast and crew as any of the characters themselves. A religious woman, Williamson made it clear that the show would be unashamedly about God and religious faith. Its characters would frequently talk about God and use his name. Of course, that was fine with Della Reese. She had been "all right" with God for quite a long time, she told Williamson.

Even so, Reese was nervous about returning to

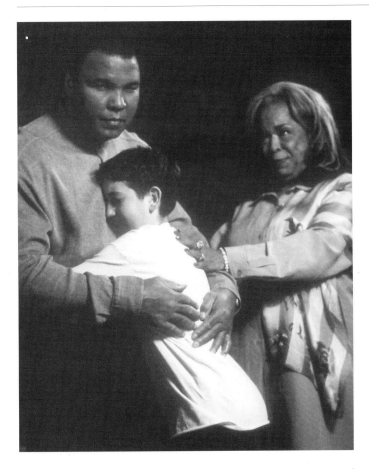

Della reluctantly began work on the program Touched By An Angel *in 1991. It has proved to be a huge success, both with its guest stars and the viewing public. Muhammed Ali and Christopher Marquette were two of the special guests on the show. Della received a star on the Hollywood Walk of Fame also in 1991.*

television after her experiences with *The Royal Family.* She realized that she would have preferred pursuing a singing career. Instead of giving up TV, however, she prayed over her choice. Before long, she knew that she should stay with the program. Everyone involved with the project believed that it probably would not have a long life—everyone except Reese, that is. It turned out that she was closer to being right about the show's prospects: despite mixed reviews, the show returned year after year. Even guest stars invited to tape individual episodes did not want to see it end. A group of them contributed funds to run what they called an "angel ad" that promoted the program. That year, Della Reese received another "heavenly" reward: a star of her own on the Hollywood Walk of Fame.

The 1995–1996 season was a turning point for the program that everyone was now calling the "angel show." During the third season, actor John Dye joined the cast as Andrew, the angel of death, who offered viewers a creative vision of what death could be like. Della Reese jokes that because of his skill in portraying the character, Dye is unfortunately not a very welcome passenger on airplanes.

Since her initial success as Tess on *Touched by an Angel*, Della Reese has received several offers to appear in TV and feature films. In addition, she has recorded the voice for a character in the animated feature film *Dinosaur* (2000). But it seems now that regardless of any other roles she takes on, she has essentially "become" Tess for many of her devoted fans. People stop her in airports or other public places to tell her how much the show and her character's beliefs have helped them. For Della Reese, one can do no better than that: she feels honored to be a part of a program that has such a wonderful effect on its viewers.

It is not only fans of the show who praise Della Reese for her role in *Touched by an Angel*. Beginning in 1996, she has been honored annually with an NAACP Image Award for Outstanding Actress in a Drama Series. The Image Awards are given to people of all races whom the judges believe have helped promote positive role models for people of color. When asked how she has accomplished so many things in her lifetime, Della Reese always has the same answer: "It's a God thing," she explains.

Della Reese is so beloved by so many people that she seems to have "family" wherever she travels. With or without her husband, children, and grandchildren, whether on the set of a television show or working in her church, Reese seems to be a "mama" to nearly all of those who love her. And what

advice does "mama" have for young people? "Hold onto your dream," she says simply. "Dreams do come true. Find something you like to do so much you would do it even if you weren't paid for it, something that the joy of it is all that makes you love to do it."

"Just as there have been angels along the way to watch over me," she says, "there are angels watching over you. Allow yourself to be as wonderful as you already are." And Della Reese, the "angel expert," ought to know.

The strong emotions of the situations and characters explored on Touched By An Angel *affect many who see the program. And viewers are often eager to share their own experiences and feelings with the stars. For this reason, Della has 'family' where ever she goes. Della appeared on "Legends of the Blues: In Performance at the White House" with President Clinton in 1999.*

CHRONOLOGY

—— ❧ ——

1931	Deloreese Patricia Early is born on July 6
1934	Develops rheumatic fever
1937	Meets older brother Rufus David (R.D.)
1943	Deloreese's cousin is killed during race riots in Detroit
1944	Deloreese joins Mahalia Jackson on summer tour through the South
1948	Graduates from Northeastern High School in Detroit
1949	Nellie Early, Deloreese's mother, dies; Deloreese marries Vermont Taliaferro
1951	Takes on name Della Reese while performing in small nightclubs in Detroit; divorces Vermont; wins "Detroit's favorite young singer" contest; lands a gig at the Flame Showbar
1952	Records her first records, which are played locally in Detroit and Chicago
1953	Hires Lee Magid as manager
1954	Records "In the Still of the Night" with Jubilee Records
1957	Records "And That Reminds Me," her first gold record; makes her first appearance on *The Ed Sullivan Show*; is voted Most Promising Young Singer of 1957
1958	Marries accountant Leroy Gray and files for divorce shortly after
1959	Richard Early, Della's father, dies; Little Deloreese is born to R.D. and Delores
1960	Gold record "Don't You Know" earns Della a Grammy nomination for Best Female Vocalist
1962	Della adopts Deloreese as her daughter
1969	Debuts her own TV show, *Della*
1976	Lands role on acclaimed TV show *Chico and the Man*
1978	Develops relationship with Franklin Lett
1979	Meets her spiritual mentor, Reverend Johnnie Coleman

1980	Suffers from a life-threatening aneurysm while performing on *The Tonight Show*, undergoes two surgeries
1983	Marries Franklin Lett
1987	Receives Grammy Award nomination for Best Female Soloist in Gospel Music; receives Emmy Award nomination for her work on *Nightmare in Badham County*; starts her own church in Los Angeles
1991	Stars in television series *The Royal Family*
1994	Takes on the role of Tess in CBS's *Touched by an Angel*; Della's star is added to the Hollywood Walk of Fame
1996–2000	Della wins five consecutive NAACP Image Awards for Outstanding Actress in a Drama Series (*Touched by an Angel*)

ACCOMPLISHMENTS

Filmography

1958	*Let's Rock*
1972	*The Voyage of the Yes* (TV movie)
1974	*Twice in a Lifetime* (TV movie)
1975	*Psychic Killer* *Cop on the Beat* (TV movie)
1976	*Nightmare in Badham County* (TV movie)
1979	*Roots: The Next Generations* (TV mini-series)
1989	*Harlem Nights*
1990	*The Kid Who Loved Christmas* (TV movie)
1992	*You Must Remember This* (TV movie)
1996	*A Thin Line Between Love and Hate*
1997	*A Match Made in Heaven*
1997	*Miracle in the Woods* (TV movie)
1998	*Emma's Wish*
1999	*The Secret Path* (TV movie) *Having Our Say: The Delaney Sisters' First 100 Years* (TV movie) *Journey to a Hate-Free Millennium* (narrator) *Anya's Bell* (TV movie)
2000	*The Moving of Sophie Myles* (TV movie) *Dinosaur* (voice of Eema)

Discography

1957	*And That Reminds Me* *Melancholy Baby*
1958	*Amen* *Date with Della Reese*
1958	*The Story of the Blues*

1959	*What Do You Know About Love?*
	Not One Minute More
	Don't You Know?
1960	*Della*
	Della by Starlight
1961	*Della Della Cha-Cha-Cha*
	Special Delivery
1962	*1962 Live Guard Session & At Basin St. East Jazz Band*
	Della Reese on Stage
	Classic Della
1963	*Waltz with Me*
1964	*C'mon and Hear*
	Della Reese at Basin Street East
1965	*I Like It Like Dat!*
1966	*Della Reese Live*
1967	*One More Time*
1990	*And Brilliance*
1996	*And That Reminds Me: The Jubilee Years*
	Voice of an Angel
1997	*Angel Sings*
	Best Thing for You Jasmine
1998	*The Collection*
	The Jubilee Years: The Singles 1954–1959
	Story of the Blues/Della at Mr. Kelly's West Side
	My Soul Feels Better Right Now
1999	*Classic Della*

FURTHER READING

Books and Articles

Boyer, Horace Clarence. *How Sweet the Sound: The Golden Age of Gospel.* Washington, D.C.: Elliot & Clark Publishing, 1995.

"Heaven Help Us!" *People*, September 22, 1999.

Hine, Darlene Clark, et.al. *Black Women in America: An Historical Encyclopedia*, vol. 2. New York: Carlson Publishing, Inc., 1993.

Pendle, Karin, ed. *Women and Music: A History.* Indianapolis, Ind.: Indiana University Press, 1991.

Rader, Dotson. "'I Knew God Would Never Let Me Down,'" *Parade*, December 17, 2000.

Reese, Della, et. al. *Angels Along the Way: My Life with Help from Above.* New York: Berkeley Boulevard Books, 1997.

Reese, Della. *God Inside of Me.* New York: Jump at the Sun/Hyperion, 1999.

———. *Strength Is the Energy of God.* Charlottesville, Virg.: Hampton Roads Publishing Co., 2001.

———. *What Is This Thing Called Love?* Charlottesville, Virg.: Hampton Roads Publishing Co., 2001.

Websites

Della Reese *People* Profile
   http://people.aol.com/people/pprofiles/dreese/credits.html

Gospel Music Hall of Fame and Museum
   http://www.gmhf.org

Newsnet—Interview with Della Reese
   http://www.newsnet5.com/sh/entertainment/ontheset/entertainment-ontheset-20001002-113329.html

Touched by an Angel Homepage
   http://www.touched.com

Unda-USA—Gabriel Awards Report
   http://www.undausa.org/gabriel.htm

INDEX

PICTURE CREDITS

TANYA DEAN holds a B.A. in history from Wittenberg University. She is an executive editor at SRA/McGraw-Hill Publishing, as well as a children's book writer and conference speaker. Previously, Mrs. Dean taught high school history and English for twelve years before entering the field of publishing. She was vice-president and publisher of Pages Publishing Group, a children's book publishing company that created books for school book fairs. She was also managing editor of a nationally known teen magazine. Tanya is the author of seventeen children's books, including a middle grade book about the history of Ohio. She lives in Springfield, Ohio, with her husband and three sons.

NATHAN IRVIN HUGGINS, one of America's leading scholars in the field of black studies, helped select the titles for the BLACK AMERICANS OF ACHIEVEMENT series, for which he also served as senior consulting editor. He was the W. E. B. DuBois Professor of History and Afro-American Studies at Harvard University and the director of the W. E. B. DuBois Institute for Afro-American Research at Harvard. He received his doctorate from Harvard in 1962 and returned there as professor in 1980 after teaching at Columbia University, the University of Massachusetts, Lake Forest College, and the California State University, Long Beach. He was the author of four books and dozens of articles, including *Black Odyssey: The Afro-American Ordeal in Slavery*, *The Harlem Renaissance*, and *Slave and*

DATE DUE

921
REE   Dean, Tanya
Della Reese

WALTRIP HIGH SCHOOL LIBRARY